9.10.21

For Rosie —
Thank you for all
your great work,
Best, RM

PORTRAITS OF RACIAL JUSTICE

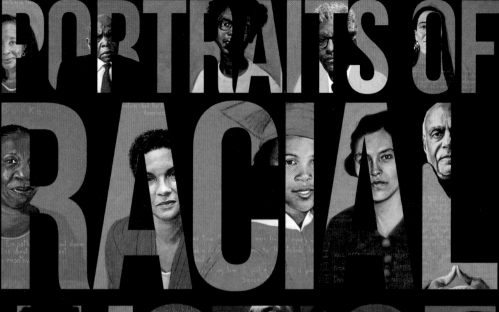

Americans Who Tell the Truth

Robert Shetterly

**With Essays by Ai-jen Poo, Dave Zirin, Sherri Mitchell,
and Rev. Lennox Yearwood,Jr.**

www.americanswhotellthetruth.org
Americans Who Tell The Truth, Inc. is a 501(c)(3) non-profit organization

Published in the United States by New Village Press
bookorders@newvillagepress.net
www.newvillagepress.org
New Village Press is a public-benefit, nonprofit publisher

Distributed by NYU Press

ISBN: 978-1-61332-163-8
Library of Congress Cataloging-in-Publication Data
Names: Shetterly, Robert, artist.
Title: Portraits of racial justice / Robert Shetterly.
Description: First edition. | New York : New Village Press, 2021. | Series:
Americans who tell the truth ; volume 1 | Summary: "The first volume of
Robert Shetterly's Americans Who Tell The Truth book series, "Portraits
of Racial Justice" is a selection of Shetterly's full-color paintings of
"truth tellers" who have advocated for the equality and dignity of all
people. Starting with Michelle Alexander and ending with Dave Zirin,
the diverse array of fifty portraits spans multiple generations and
struggles. In addition to accompanying descriptions of each subject's
accomplishments, this volume includes four original opening essays
on racial justice in the United States"— Provided by publisher.
Identifiers: LCCN 2021012748 | ISBN 9781613321638 (hardback)
Subjects: LCSH: United States—Race relations. | Social reformers—
United States—Portraits. | Social reformers—United States—
Biography. | Racial justice—United States.
Classification: LCC E184.A1 S5746 2021 | DDC 305.800973--dc23
LC record available at https://lccn.loc.gov/2021012748

Publication Date: September, 2021
First Edition

Author photo by Richard Kane
Cover design by Kevin Stone
Interior design and composition by Leigh McLellan Design

These are portraits of citizens of
a country that does not yet exist.
—Bill Ayers

• • •

This book is dedicated to all those
who have worked so hard for the equal
and essential dignity of all human beings.

Contents

Preface

I have a friend who has been visiting the standing stones found all around the British Isles and Brittany. Most of us are familiar with Stonehenge, but there are a thousand more. They date from the Neolithic and Bronze Ages, four to five thousand years ago. My friend maintains that the first human creative act was to stand up a stone.

Why is that?

When a stone is stood up, its role changes. It's individuated; it ritualizes its space. It calls the residents of the area to be in relation to it—it creates an address in place and time.

A person who stands up with moral courage against injustice affects a community's morality the same way a stone does the geography. That person creates an address for truth and justice in history, a center for others to rally around, creates resistance, value, and dignity.

William Sloane Coffin, Jr., said, "Socrates had it wrong; it is not the unexamined but finally the uncommitted life that is not worth living." We remember, and are taught by, the illiterate former slave Sojourner Truth, not the well-to-do white woman whose house she cleaned. Sojourner's committed passion for abolition and women's rights defines the ethical address we want to call home. There is a kind of meaning, a claim to stature, in our lives that can only be purchased with courage.

Muhammad Ali refusing to fight in an imperialist, racist war; Barbara Johns demanding an equal education; James Baldwin patiently explaining to white people the invidious humiliations of white privilege; Bree Newsome taking down the Confederate flag in South Carolina—all of them standing stones. All of the portraits in this book are standing stones for racial justice.

Standing-up people mark the path of justice and morality in an otherwise baffling and trackless historical landscape. They map the growth of meaning in our lives. They narrate the story of equality and dignity. Without them, both our consciousness and our conscience cannot evolve beyond the manipulations of power. Power tries to dismiss them, marginalize them, discredit them, and imprison them because the moral courage of standing people exposes the weakness of unjust power. Without them, justice has no heartbeat. The original human creative act is to be a standing stone.

• • •

I've asked several of the portrait subjects in this book to write essays about racial justice today. Their thoughts are as diverse as the people themselves: Ai-jen Poo, founder of the National Domestic Workers Alliance, writes about the lives and organizing strength of domestic workers and women; Rev. Yearwood, head of the Hip Hop Caucus, explains how the only way to evolve a truly peaceful, nonracist democratic society is by cultivating nonviolence, courage, and conscience; sports journalist Dave Zirin shows how the sports world is a microcosm and battleground of the racist and sexist injustices in our society; and Sherri Mitchell, author and Indigenous rights activist, dissects the deep history of white supremacy.

This book is an art book, a history book, a guidebook, a curriculum, a manifesto. It is a community of people unafraid to name the failures of this country and the injustices of power that benefit from those failures. These truth tellers define the way forward.

This book has no interest in discriminations of ethnicity or color, left or right, red or blue, young or old, gender distinction, religions, or belief systems. This book insists on the equality and dignity of all people; it insists on a moral and political society that promotes those values. This book celebrates the struggle toward a just and beloved community.

I decided to arrange the portraits alphabetically. I tried arranging them by chronology and by issue. However, since the overriding issue of racial justice is persistent across time, for ease of reference, alphabetically seemed best. That arrangement meant, then, that Michelle Alexander's portrait and quote would be first. She says, "Our task is to end . . . the history and cycle of caste in America." And it meant that Dave Zirin's would be last. He says, "Racism is not about hurtful words, bruised feelings, political correctness . . . Racism is about the power to treat entire groups of people as something less than human—for the benefit of that power." Between that task and that definition is the entire struggle for racial justice.

In part, I have painted the portraits to honor the courage and persistence of people who insist that America live up to its own ideals. But primarily I have painted them to be models of courageous citizenship.

Robert Shetterly
Brooksville, Maine
March 2021

Essays on
Social Justice

When Systems Fail, Women of Color Lead

Ai-jen Poo

I was raised by strong, caring women who worked hard and weren't afraid of struggle. They were critical sources of care for many people around them, capable of overcoming any obstacle. They knew their power and the value of their contributions and didn't fear failure. In fact, they taught me that failure is important to growth and developing strength.

As a young girl, this was hard to understand. We seek out the success of the heroes in our lives. But my heroes—my mother and grandmother—taught me that it is our moments of failure that often help us become stronger. This became critical to how I understood the world. Failure—whether I experienced it personally or identified it in our systems, policies, and institutions—became moments of opportunity, when I learned what we must change and what new models must be built.

As a child, I lived in Taiwan with my grandmother, a trained nurse, and soaked up her life lessons, from the way she cared for my sister and me as infants to the care she showed the many people who sought treatment at her clinic. Her role as a caregiver was deeply respected.

My mother became a doctor and embarked on a career in medicine, caring for people with terminal cancer. She taught me the importance of care at every stage of life. I saw how care changed and connected all those who gave and received it; it was a bonding force, and as a young girl, it seemed the most important work anyone could do.

However, growing up was a process of learning the many ways that women are both powerful and disempowered by the systems of our society. Even as the power of women was undeniable, I began to see where culture and policy have failed women. The older I got, the more I understood that while women were caring for families, working, and powering so much of our society, they were rarely in positions of power and decision making themselves.

As a young adult living in New York City, I volunteered at a domestic violence hotline, taking calls from women in crisis, many of whom had jobs caring for others' children and families as domestic workers. These women were incredibly strong. Working in low-wage service jobs, often for long hours, didn't allow them to move out of an unsafe living situation or properly care for their children. Often, the women on the other end of the hotline were undocumented immigrants, fearful that seeking help would put them at risk of deportation and separation from their children. Their struggles often extended beyond the violence in their homes to experiencing racially motivated abuse, wage theft, and sexual assault from their employers.

This experience showed me the many profound ways the lives and contributions of women, especially women of color, have been devalued. Although I was introduced to care as the most important work we do, the economy has devalued this work as "women's work" and deemed it unskilled, when we know it is anything but. As an occupation, this work has always been done by women in the margins of the economy. Some of the first domestic workers were enslaved Black women, and today the work is still disproportionately done by Black and other women of color, including large numbers of undocumented immigrant women. Simultaneously, this workforce, still referred to as "help," has faced systematic exclusion from basic labor rights and protections and remains undervalued and unsupported.

And yet, since the days of following my grandmother around, I have been consistently struck by the undeniable power of women and the responsibility women too often shoulder alone to care for their families from birth to death. Whenever there is a crisis, women show up. When our health care is at risk, women pack congressional town hall meetings to protect it. When a sexual predator was elected president of the United States in 2016, I joined millions of women to march on Washington. When our democracy was under assault with new forms of voter suppression and disinformation, Black women ran for office, organized, and voted in unprecedented numbers to save our democracy in 2020.

My experiences lead me to imagine a world where Black women, other women of color, and domestic workers have the power to govern and lead the fight for changes in our policy and systems. Thankfully, the domestic worker movement is making real progress, following the leadership of women of color who are stepping forward in this moment to share their stories and fight for what they deserve—women like Allison Julien, a domestic worker for more than twenty-five years.

I first met Allison almost twenty years ago in a park in New York City, when she was working as a nanny. I had just begun organizing domestic workers. As I got to know Allison, an immigrant from Barbados, I learned that her mother and grandmother were also domestic workers. Allison became a leader in the domestic worker movement, and on July 15, 2019, she joined one hundred other domestic workers in Washington, D.C., to support the introduction of a National Domestic Workers Bill of Rights, introduced by Congresswoman Pramila Jayapal and then-Senator Kamala Harris, now vice president of the United States. Women of color fighting alongside those in elected positions for the legislative protections they deserve is the reality these women have fought to create.

Allison and I are part of a growing movement to value all the work that happens in our care economy, ensuring that every worker whose job it is to care for us—from the nanny to the home-care worker—earns a family-sustaining wage, with real economic opportunity; that every person, across his or her life span, has the care and support needed to live a full life. Rosalynn Carter famously said, "There are only four kinds of people in the world: those who have been caregivers, those who are currently caregivers, those who will be caregivers, and those who will need caregivers." While the way we live is changing more and more rapidly, our need for care has remained—and will remain—constant.

While our movement has been fighting for this respect and dignity for generations, it took a pandemic to firmly establish the idea that we need to value and protect the work that goes into caring for our families. Women have struggled to work from home, if they can, while helping their children learn remotely. Families have rushed to evacuate elderly loved ones from nursing homes and find the right care for them in their homes. Simultaneously, domestic workers' incomes have been devastated, as domestic work, by definition, can not be done from home, and most domestic workers, not having a formal contract in place, have found themselves without work, having received no notice. The crisis that has forced us into our homes has revealed the crisis that already existed for people working in others' homes.

The task of rebuilding following the pandemic will be an opportunity to reset our systems, learn from our failures, and make the corrections that our economy and society need. The urgency of the moment is fierce. With women of color leading at every level, I believe we can and must rise to the occasion, because we will never lose sight of who our superheroes are. Women are capable of anything and necessary for everything.

Sports, Race, and Politics

Dave Zirin

Those who say that sports and politics don't mix and that athletes should just "shut up and dribble" are doing more than betraying their own ignorance. Their aversion is not to "sports and politics," but to sports and a certain kind of politics: the politics of resistance. I can't imagine the early years of the civil rights movement without referencing Jackie Robinson; nor can I talk about the 1960s without bringing up Muhammad Ali. And there is no full accounting of the women's movement without Billie Jean King. The struggle of these athletes, not to mention thousands of others who have used their platform to speak truth to power, creates a template for how we can remake the sports world as a citadel for justice.

To understand why this task is so pressing, I believe we must first understand where we are. Only then can we create a vision of a sports landscape unfettered by the muck of our present moment. Currently, the sports world is a morass of inequality and injustice. At the youth level, roughly 70 percent of children in this country stop playing organized sports by the age of thirteen. Burdened by the expectations of frustrated adults, they say, "It's just not fun anymore." Their first act of rebellion is choosing not to play. For girls, the percentage of dropouts is even higher, as the pressure not to play becomes tied up with gender expectations, homophobia, or unequal access. That means removing themselves from an environment that might have been a setting for growth, friendship, and community. But it's not. In too many communities, it's a cauldron of angst, where kids are tracked into one of two groups: those who get to play and those who are told to watch. I want to have a sports world with expanded recess and daily physical education for young people so that they aren't raised to be alienated from the idea of play. I want to have a sports world where girls and nonbinary folk find the space to compete, frolic, and enjoy.

At the collegiate level, I see players—in theory, "student athletes"—who find themselves in a position of indentured servitude. Deemed "essential workers" during the COVID-19 pandemic, they have none of the rights or pay of the campus workers that they undoubtedly are. Then there is the racism that narrows opportunities for Black athletes and keeps coaching positions as well as executive positions and professional franchise ownership largely white. And even though we have seen progress, the wallowing of teams on every level of sports in Native American mascotry continues. I want to see a college sports system that does not reek of injustice, an injustice that rests primarily on the shoulders of the Black athletes who play the revenue-producing sports of football and basketball.

I want a sports world where franchise owners pay for their own stadiums. We should not be taxed for the playpens of billionaires—playpens that many of us could not afford to enter even though we financed the damn things. In fact, a sports world without owners at all would be most welcome. Imagine if *we the people* ran sports teams in our own interests. If that sounds outlandish, just look at the Green Bay Packers, a fan-owned life raft for a community, rather than the financial albatross around the neck of most host cities.

But the sports world will not change in a vacuum. That will require real movements and masses of people marching outside of the stadiums where we go to forget the troubles that surround us. When those struggles do take place, they have the capacity to ricochet into the sports world in absolutely electric fashion. We saw this in 2020, when the multiracial masses of people taking to the streets following the police murder of George Floyd led to NBA and WNBA player protests. Or when Colin Kaepernick tweeted, "When civility leads to death, revolting is the only logical reaction. The cries for peace will rain down, and when they do, they will land on deaf ears, because your violence has brought this resistance. We have the right to fight back!"

Athletes marched with the people and took their own demands for racial justice to the commissioners and franchise owners in the sports world. It is no coincidence that in the wake of these marches I finally saw what many of us thought we might never see: the changing of the racist name of the Washington football team. We also saw new demands by players that teams take up the issue of racial and social equity in their communities. Players demanded that the teams involve themselves in social justice work: fighting for police reform, taking a stand against racism, and opening up stadiums as voting centers for the November 2020 elections.

I also saw pro athletes take the struggle beyond even the movement in the streets last August, when players across the sports landscape went on strike for Black lives, following the police shooting of Jacob Blake in Kenosha, Wisconsin. As Milwaukee Bucks guard George Hill said, "Until the world gets their shit together, I guess we're not going to get our stuff together." History will record that it was athletes who brought the question of labor and strikes into the struggle for Black lives.

These movements, strikes, and struggles do more than fight for social justice in the past and present. They paint a vision of what exactly a future sports world could look like. I believe if sports are ever going to be something other than what they are, we need to dare to dream about and envision what they could be.

Sports have tragically, at times, proved to be a toxic part of our culture. But take a moment and consider with me the idea that the best of sports— the teamwork, the ability to break down boundaries between people, the exercise, the fun—might be universal in every locker room. Imagine if that were the expectation instead of the unique, singular experience. Imagine if coaches used sports to build understanding about social justice and fighting bigotry. What if your team were a place where winning wasn't the only thing, but instead a vehicle for personal growth and societal uplift? That is a sports world, not to mention a real world, I hope to see.

Eradicating Racism:
The Threat of Inclusion in an Exclusionary World

Sherri Mitchell, Weh'na Ha'mu Kwasset

The last four hundred years of racial "science" have proved one thing—that dividing human beings into racial categories has no basis in science. It is nothing more than white confirmation bias dissembling as science. Despite its lack of legitimacy, this faux science has been used effectively to influence the social, political, economic, and cultural discourse that has shaped our most exclusionary societies. And it has been key in blocking any attempts at eradicating racism and moving us toward greater equity and justice.

As Penawahpskewe,[1] I am a survivor of that science and all its resultant violence—I have survived the Indian wars, the massacres, the forced-march removals, the rapes and baby stealings. I have survived starvation and disease, and bounties placed upon the bloody skins of my people. I have survived genocide, ethnic cleansing, and conquest. I have survived "discovery," the invisibility of *terra nullius,* and papal bulls that sought to vanquish me. To this day, my skin is coated red with the blood of that science, because its fallacy has never been relegated to the past, but remains a living, breathing expression of this country's ongoing hypocrisy.

In recent years we have witnessed a significant rise in racial violence in the United States. The Department of Homeland Security's 2019 report notes that white supremacists pose the largest domestic terror threat in the United States. The Anti-Defamation League has also reported that right-wing extremists, with ties to white supremacy, have committed nearly all the extremist crimes in the United States since 2017. Many people attribute the disturbing rise in racial violence in the United States to the Trump administration's public sanctioning of white supremacist rhetoric and to that president's complete unwillingness to condemn racial violence. However, that dismisses the structural racism that has perpetuated racial inequity across time by disproportionately favoring the privilege of whiteness. The current rise in hate speech and increased racial violence is simply the expected backlash against contemporary challenges to the well-defined apparatus of structural racism and the systems it upholds.

The rise in violence against marginalized people is growing in direct proportion to their increased visibility and import in decision-making positions. For centuries, white people have held the default position in this country. Today, that appears to be changing and white people are experiencing the discomfort of a shifting social paradigm where their voices are not automatically centered and their authority (morally, legally, and politically) is not automatically accepted.

The violent behaviors that we have witnessed in the United States in recent years can all be categorized as a backlash against inclusion. The immigration scare is less about the danger at our southern border than it is about the exclusion of people of color from entering this country and tipping the scales toward a non-white majority. The ban on transgender people in the military is not truly about increased costs; it is simply about the exclusion of those who are defying deeply entrenched heteronormative gender roles. And the attack on women's bodily rights by the GOP is simply a backlash against the greater inclusion of women, specifically women of color, in Congress, an arena that has for centuries been reserved for white men.

We also see in-group dynamics that highlight the fact that inclusion is the threat being faced. We saw it

1. Penawahpskewe refers to the people of the Penawahpskek (Penobscot) Nation.

in the Women's March when white women were criticized for having a lack of representation from women of color. In response to this criticism, the white organizers stated that these "attacks" on white women were the inevitable outcome of intersectionality, and they intended to fight back. This clearly indicates that intersectionality (inclusion) is viewed as a threat to the status and power that is held by white women. This isn't new; it goes all the way back to the women's suffrage movement, where white women fought for the vote, but only for those who looked like them. As a result, white women got the right to vote in 1920, but Black and Indigenous women had to wait another half century to receive that same right.

Given that social inclusion is essential to human well-being, it is easy to understand how an entire society can be psychologically damaged by ingrained systems of exclusion. Members of an exclusionary society often lack the emotional skills required for coping with changes to their social status, because the expectation is that their status will last indefinitely. This can result in disproportionate reactions to changes in one's social environment, especially changes that impact the default status of those in power. A clear example of this is having the election of the first Black president followed by white supremacists and neo-Nazis marching through the streets carrying burning torches.

The way to move our current societies from exclusion to inclusion may appear to be simply providing greater participation for those who have historically been excluded. However, this belief assumes that mainstream society is legitimate and that inclusion into this society is beneficial or even desirable to all. This may not be the case.

I once heard Frances Moore Lappé ask a group of environmentalists, "Why are we together creating a world that we as individuals would never choose?"

This simple question offers us two critical inquiries: (1) what is the true depth and breadth of our co-creative capabilities, and (2) what type of world would we choose for ourselves and those we love? If we want to move toward a new society and begin establishing a new way of being in relationship with one another, then we must be willing to admit that the society that exists is purposely inequitable, and that it is built on a structure that supports that inequity and is therefore beyond repair. Furthermore, we must have the courage to envision collectively the world that we most want to inhabit and then go about the hard work of actively creating that reality. This work will require committed antiracist persistence, which means that we will have to dissolve the foundations of exclusion that this country was built upon, while simultaneously incorporating deliberate and active practices of inclusion.

Inclusion is the default instinct of our specific humanoid species. It is the very thing that allowed us to survive and flourish when all other humanoid species became extinct. The deeply ingrained practices of exclusion that are embedded into our current systems are unnatural. They are adaptation strategies brought about by inequitable colonial systems that were built on distorted ideologies of racial superiority and unchecked greed. These systemic inequities harm all members of society by diminishing the flow of creative intelligence and problem-solving capabilities that would benefit us all. It is well past the time for us to eradicate these inequitable systems and begin building more humane systems and structures. This means that we must wake up to the truth of who we are in this moment—we are the bridge between an exclusionary past and an inclusive future. The only way to reach the other side is by provoking a yearning within individual hearts for the inclusive world that we can only create collectively.

The World We Seek Is Within Us

Rev. Lennox Yearwood, Jr.

The year 2020 may go down in history as one of the deadliest years in American history. The story in the textbooks will probably read something like this: "More than nineteen thousand Americans were killed in shootings and firearm-related incidents in 2020. The Gun Violence Archive estimates that this is the highest death toll in more than twenty years—and this doesn't include gun suicides."

What will likely be left out of the textbook is the disproportionate impact this violence has had on poor Black and brown communities.

We must fight to eradicate this violence from our society.

A nonviolent society is not a new concept. Great men and women like Dr. Martin Luther King, Jr., Dorothy Day, and Gandhi have all taken action for nonviolent change.

If we are to have a world that supports racial, economic, and environmental justice, we must build a nonviolent society. Dr. Martin Luther King, Jr., said, "In the nonviolent army, there is room for everyone who wants to join up. There is no color distinction. There is no examination, no pledge . . . nonviolent soldiers are called upon to examine their greatest weapons—their heart, their conscience, their courage, and their sense of justice."

If we believe, like Dr. King, that our greatest weapons are our hearts, our conscience, our courage, and our sense of justice, then we have only to change ourselves to create the world we seek.

To create this world, the first thing we must do is create a moral foundation that makes the rights of humans more important than anything else. Our leaders and corporations must make people more valuable than profit, and make social responsibility the first priority.

Once we have established a foundation that treats people as equally human, regardless of their differences in race, ethnicity, sexual orientation, or social status, we then have to work on ourselves—our hearts, our conscience, our courage, and our sense of justice. In this work, you can't be bitter, jaded, or cynical.

Heart-Centered Work

You must clear your heart. You must allow yourself to be free from all of the burdens and entrapments of anger and hate, which block the work of peace. You must allow yourself to have a heart, not only for those you are fighting for but also for those whom you are fighting against. You must have a heart that allows you to forgive, but you must not lose sight of justice. You must have a heart that allows you to understand and feel the pain of the most vulnerable, especially the pain of those who are different from you. Your heart can't guide only you; it must also protect others.

Conscience Work

In addition to a compassionate heart, you must have a conscience that is troubled when you see injustice. Your conscience must demand that you speak out. You can't sleep or rest easy if you acknowledge the pain of humanity. Your conscience tells you that you can't turn away.

Courage Work

The next thing is your courage. We must have the determination to push on when we think we can't, and a courage that keeps us standing when the weight of the world is upon us.

I remember many years ago when we were beginning to speak out against the Keystone XL pipeline and many of my friends who worked for President Barack Obama said it was useless to oppose this pipeline project, that it was a done deal.

We had the courage to stand up to those who were in power.

We knew this pipeline was wrong and we were willing to stand up and be arrested and be prosecuted. We knew we had to have the courage to, in the words of the late, great Congressman John Lewis, get into "good trouble."

Many years have gone past, and because of that courage and our unified character, the Keystone XL pipeline will never be built, the pollution from that pipeline will never be spewed, and the contaminants of that pollution will never cause cancer or emphysema.

You must have courage to see progress.

Justice Work

The last thing is a sense of justice. Being just means that we are acting according to what is morally right and fair. We must consider what is best for everyone, not just for those who are like us. We must fight for racial and economic health and for climate justice, which holds us all accountable for treating everyone with humanity.

We live in a time when we have no choice but to choose justice.

The World We Seek Is Within Us

If we operate using these principles, we will win. If we operate using these principles, our nation and our world will change. We must use these weapons to dismantle all of the things that are harming our communities. It won't be easy, because when we face violence, we want to respond with violence; but we

must respond with nonviolence and operate using these principles.

We are dealing with so many difficult things at once: the economy; the pandemic; the triple injustices of race, climate, and environment. Unchecked, these injustices will destroy us. We are literally fighting for our existence. Now is the time for us all—Black, white, brown, all genders, *humans*—to create a world that can overcome all these obstacles.

Our world is based not only on physical violence but on the violence of extraction and white supremacy. Violent resistance does not work. Even for those with privilege, resources, and an abundance of money, it still does not bring justice. The only thing that can heal us and move us forward is nonviolence.

We are at what I call the "lunch counter moment" for the twenty-first century. Just as the lunch counter sit-ins sparked the civil rights movement in 1960, we have reached that point where the pressure to change is much greater than the pressure to stay the same, and we are responding. The violent events of 2020 pushed us to this tipping point. We have to change the narrative. When we finally establish a nonviolent, human-centered society, we will not only survive; we will thrive.

We have a long way to go. But I believe we are beginning to build this beloved community, the world where all people will be treated with equity and fairness. We must continue to push, do the work to align our hearts and conscience with the words of the Declaration, which say we are all created equal. Then we must live in that spirit. The beauty of this is, as Dr. King said, that everyone can do it. No one person is more qualified than another. Let's do this work together. The world we seek is within us. All POWER TO THE PEOPLE!

The Song of Justice

Robert Shetterly

There's a fifty-acre woods behind my home in rural Maine, a raggedy woods, an unprepossessing mix of pine, spruce, oak, ash, and birch, including many dead trees—all of which I find beautiful. The soil is shallow and poor. Tree roots thickly vein the paths, making the walking awkward. The plentiful mosses and ferns, though, remain green even in January. I go there when I'm down, particularly to get to one spot. About a half mile into the woods and seventy-five feet (I've paced it off) from a little rocky brook that winds out through a sphagnum bog before dropping into a ravine toward the river, I begin to hear it—the rippling, gurgling, splashing of living water. That sound, the voice of that running water falling, pooling, trickling, begins to lift away whatever gnarly angst has grabbed hold of me. The sound of that water restores my life.

This morning as I approached the brook and first heard the watery murmur singing to itself, I realized I had begun painting the *Americans Who Tell the Truth* portraits to have an effect on me similar to that brook's song. In 2001 and 2002, as the George W. Bush administration propagandized and lied about the necessity of attacking Iraq as a response to 9/11, I was feeling more and more angry, depressed, and alienated. Another criminal war of imperialism! Hundreds of thousands of innocent people about to die! Another bonanza for the war profiteers! What to do? How to feel unsullied simply being an American?

What I chose was to exorcize the shameful liars who were colonizing my head and heart and replace them with portraits of Americans who made me feel proud of this country and its tortuous journey to live up to its own ideals. I wanted to hear the rippling spring of that history—its courage, its perseverance, its idealism—as it flowed out of the cotton fields, the prisons, the coal mines and steel mills, as it poured out of the segregated cities and towns and schools, and rained down on the oblivious status quo. I wanted to see where the streams ran into the rivers, and the rivers to the sea. I wanted to be healed of the crimes of this country, baptized in the legacy of its struggle toward justice. I painted Frederick Douglass. I painted Sojourner Truth. I painted Harriet Tubman. I painted Howard Zinn and John Brown, Eugene Debs, Anne Braden, and Rosa Parks. I realized I didn't need the babbling sound of a brook; what I needed was the cascade of a river. I painted 250 people who told truth to power, who marched and preached and protested, who committed civil disobedience, who went to jail, who died for justice—all so that some powerful language about unalienable rights, written by slave owners, would be true for them.

I paint with my fingers, building up thin layers of color, then wiping them away, drawing out skin tones from underneath by varying the pressure. Sometimes my painting process is more like sculpture than painting, my fingers shaping eyes and noses, ears and mouths. It's intensely intimate. Even though it's a process of extreme seeing, it's as if I'm a blind person feeling for contours of character and integrity. It's like falling in love. And each person I paint creates a unique verse in the song of this country. Each person inspires and fortifies in a new way.

When I painted Sojourner Truth, she explained to me why this project was necessary. She was in Ohio in the 1850s on a lecture tour with a cohort of abolitionists and women's rights advocates. She fixed me with her stern 150-year-old stare and said, "Now I hears talkin' about de Constitution and de rights of man. I comes up and takes hold of dis Constitution. It looks mighty big, and I feels for my rights, but der aint any dare. Den I says, God, what ails dis Constitution? He says to me, 'Sojourner, der is a little weasel in it.'"

Sojourner said she took hold of this mighty big Constitution and felt for her rights, but to no avail. It's as though, for her, the Constitution was a big hairy creature that, like a Saint Bernard dog, was supposed to deliver some saving balm that she would find hidden in its fur. She felt for her rights. Nothing. Instead, she rousted out the weasel. If I were to attribute one vocation, one common mission, to every one of these portraits, it's the pursuit of that weasel. It's as elusive as the well-greased lawyer of an oil company. Some mighty powerful and clever people keep finding secret new dens for it to burrow in. We are all taught to extol the power of this country, its economic power, its military power, the power of its ideals. It's a shock to discover that one of its greatest powers is in the stinginess with which it withholds rights and freedoms from its own people, how cleverly it weasels out of counting some people's votes, how it has built systems of elite wealth and privilege, poverty and exclusion based in the earliest inequalities, which persist until today, how adamantly it embraces socialism . . . for the rich, and for the white.

I visited Bozeman, Montana, and spoke with five hundred students in the Chief Joseph Middle School. I was pleased that the school had been named for this great Nez Perce chief, but I was impressed more by the irony. Chief Joseph achieved his fame leading hundreds of hungry, cold Native Americans on an exhausting, deadly strategic retreat from the U.S. Cavalry, trying to escape into Canada to avoid being forced onto a reservation. To name the school for him was similar to naming a housing development Woodland Acres after clear-cutting the trees to build the houses.

I read the students the chief's quote I'd scratched into the portrait: "I have asked some of the great white chiefs where they get their authority to say to the Indian that he shall stay in one place, while he sees white men going where they please. They cannot tell me." And then I asked them where this white authority came from. Hands shot up. "Power," the kids said. "Yes," I said, "but what gave them power?"

"Guns," they said. "And why did they think they had the right to move the Indians off their own land?" "Racism," they said. "And why couldn't the U.S. soldiers explain this to Chief Joseph?" "Because their power and racism seemed right to them." "Okay, but why did they move them?" "They wanted the Indians' land." These kids were very astute. They had learned some wisdom about the nature of race and power and imperialism from Chief Joseph. The school was indeed named correctly; the chief was not gone.

Painting Muhammad Ali helped me understand the difference between moral and physical courage. When Ali climbed into the ring to fight Sonny Liston or Joe Frazier, his physical courage was celebrated. When he refused the military draft for the Vietnam War, outraged people called him a traitor and a coward. He was teaching us, then, a more complicated and harder kind of courage—moral. Everyone celebrates physical courage; unjust power fears and denounces moral courage. When I am in a school, after telling kids the story about how after Ali refused the military draft and had his world heavyweight title taken away and he was prohibited from fighting for over four years while in his prime, I ask them, "What did he have left?" Someone will say tentatively, "His dignity?" Another person will say, "His self-respect?" Muhammad Ali's moral courage was contagious. Thousands of draft-age young men—like me!—said to themselves, If he can do that and lose so much, certainly I, too, can refuse to fight in an immoral war. Many of the portraits are of people whom I turned to for courage when I was unsure what to do; many of them I didn't know about until I began this project, and turn to now.

In 1964, my older brother Jay joined the Student Nonviolent Coordinating Committee (SNCC) and went—despite the shocked disapproval of our parents—to rural Mississippi as part of Freedom Summer to help register Black Americans to vote. I asked him to explain what was going on. He said, "Read James Baldwin." I give the same advice today to anyone who wants to understand the history of racism in this country, especially to anyone who wants to understand what it feels like to be the object of persistent racism. Baldwin said, "To be a Negro in this country and to be relatively conscious is to be in a rage almost all the time." And he counseled his nephew, "Please try to remember that what they [white people] believe, as well as what they do and cause you to endure, does not testify to your inferiority, but to their inhumanity." To really know, one must feel. Baldwin makes you feel. All the issues that are being talked about today as though newly discovered—systemic racism, white supremacy, white privilege—Baldwin was patiently and eloquently explaining to white America seventy years ago: "People who treat other people as less than human must not be surprised when the bread they have cast on the waters comes floating back to them, poisoned."

Perhaps the most inspiring of human virtues is courage. William Sloane Coffin, Jr., the white pastor who risked his life in support of civil rights, including as a freedom rider, said, "Without courage there are no other virtues." What's become obvious to me while painting these portraits and learning this history is that the person of courage becomes our teacher. In December 1955, Rosa Parks, a seamstress in Montgomery, became this nation's teacher. She taught us the daily humiliation of racism, and she taught us that the effective way to change unjust law is to commit civil disobedience: Break the law; tell the judge, "I'm not a bad person breaking a good law, but a good person breaking bad law; make the law just!"

And America may never have been blessed with a teacher more eloquent about the moral imperatives of racial justice than Martin Luther King, Jr.—unless it was Frederick Douglass, whose rhetoric resounds from the page as courageously and powerfully as Dr. King's does from recordings. What I didn't know was how much of the history of courage belongs to teenage girls. Emma Tenayuca, Barbara Johns, Claudette Colvin, Zyahna Bryant—all of them names I had never heard when I began this project—prove that the

decisive factor of inspiring leadership is neither age nor gender. It's courage. Emma Tenayuca said, "I was arrested a number of times. I never thought in terms of fear. I thought in terms of justice." And Claudette Colvin said, ". . . when it comes to justice, there is no easy way to get it. You can't sugarcoat it. You have to take a stand and say, 'This is not right.' And I did." These young women are my heroes. They are America's heroes. That I had lived more than sixty years in this country and had not heard of them reinforces the disturbing fact that when power controls the narrative, you may never hear the most important stories, stories of successful resistance to unjust power, stories that may empower and change your life.

Janice Mirikitani was only four years old when she and her family were rounded up from their California home during the World War II hysteria and imprisoned in an internment camp for Japanese Americans. The brutal racism of that experience (German Americans weren't being imprisoned) created a lifelong trauma, which she has alleviated by dedicating her adult life to reaching out to other traumatized people through her poetry and social programs. Mirikitani's passion, along with that of her husband, the Reverend Cecil Williams (also a portrait), has been to create programs for women and families as they struggle with issues of substance abuse, rape, incest, domestic violence, the AIDS crisis, single parenting, child care, health care, education, and job development. She says, "I found that my wounds begin to heal when the voices of those endangered by silence are given power. The silence of hopelessness, of despair buried in the depths of poverty, violence, racism . . . are more deadly than bullets. . . . The gift of light, in our compassion, our listening, our works of love . . . is the gift of life to ourselves."

Which makes me think of Fannie Lou Hamer. When I painted Howard Zinn's portrait—Professor Zinn is the author of A People's History of the United States and was fired from teaching at Spelman College in the early 1960s for encouraging his students to become active in civil rights—I asked him, if he were doing what I am, whom would he paint. Without hesitation, he said Fannie Lou Hamer. Ms. Hamer, the twentieth child of sharecroppers in Mississippi, joined Freedom Summer and then cofounded the Mississippi Freedom Democratic Party with Bob Moses in 1964. Earlier, in 1962, on the way home to Ruleville after having once again been refused the right to register to vote, she was arrested with a group of women and unmercifully beaten by white policemen. In so much pain she could not move, she stood all night in her cell, and as morning dawned, she began to sing. The women in the other cells joined in her singing. She said she knew then if they were going to stop her, they would have to kill her. "If I fall," she said, "I'll fall five feet four inches forward in the fight for freedom. I'm not backing off." The refusal to be intimidated is the common denominator of all the portraits.

Fannie Lou Hamer's soul-restoring singing from jail, like the sound of water rippling over rocks, is the irrepressible perfect pitch of life, the music of living defiantly for justice. It sounds the highest form of virtue there is—the courage to confront evil with the spirit of love. When one wanders into the dense and raggedy woods of our collective history and tries to find one's way to the practice and truth of our ideals, it's easy to get lost—so many false narratives, exceptionalist myths, and racist justifications. Listen for the songs of justice. They will lead you home.

The Portraits

Michelle Alexander

Professor of law, writer, historian, civil rights advocate; b. 1968

. . . the refusal and failure to recognize the dignity and humanity of ALL people has formed the sturdy foundation of every caste system that has ever existed in the United States or anywhere else. Our task is to end not just mass incarceration, but the history and cycle of caste in America.

Two years after the election of America's first African American president, Michelle Alexander published *The New Jim Crow: Mass Incarceration in the Age of Colorblindness.* Many people considered Barack Obama's election evidence that America had finally moved past race, but Alexander wrote that America needs "a radical restructuring of our economy and our society in order to ensure that poor people of all colors gain equal access to opportunity, jobs, housing, and healthcare." During a legal career focused on civil rights advocacy and antidiscrimination cases, Alexander reached the conclusion that, as a result of mass incarceration, huge numbers of African American men "are permanently locked into an inferior, second-class status, or caste, by law and custom."

Alexander graduated from Vanderbilt University, and earned a law degree from Stanford in 1992, before beginning her career as civil rights advocate. In 1998, she was hired as the founding director of the Northern California ACLU chapter's Racial Justice Project. While interviewing potential plaintiffs in a case against the Oakland Police Department, Alexander met a young man who had kept detailed notes about years of police abuse in his neighborhood. Preparing to use his testimony to move forward with the case, she learned he was a drug felon. Though he insisted he'd been framed by a police officer, Alexander knew the drug conviction could undermine his cred-

ibility in court. Angry, the young man told her that she wouldn't find anyone in his neighborhood who didn't have a record. He tore up his notes and left the office, yelling, "You're no better than the police. You're just like them. I can't believe I trusted you."

Months later, Alexander read that several police officers, including one the young man had mentioned, had been arrested for framing and beating up innocent citizens. During an interview in 2012, Alexander recalled her feelings in that moment: ". . . he's right about me. The minute he told me he was a felon, I stopped listening. . . . And I realized that my crime wasn't so much that I had refused to represent an innocent man, someone who had been telling me the truth, but that I had been blind to all those who were guilty and that their stories weren't being told." That realization planted the seed for *The New Jim Crow.*

Alexander calls the devastating impact that the War on Drugs has inflicted on African American families "the new Jim Crow" because its policies target Black men and institutionalize discrimination, as was the case during the segregationist Jim Crow laws enacted in the United States between 1877 and 1965.

Currently, Alexander is a visiting professor at Union Theological Seminary, in New York City, and writes opinion columns for *The New York Times.* She travels the country, speaking to inspire citizens to take action against mass incarceration.

...the refusal and failure to recognize the dignity and humanity of ALL people has formed the sturdy foundation of every caste system that has ever existed in the United States or anywhere else. Our task is to end not just mass incarceration, but the history and cycle of caste in America.

Michelle Alexander

Robert Shetterly
2012

Muhammad Ali

Boxer, civil rights activist, humanitarian; b. 1942, d. 2016

If I thought going to war would bring freedom and equality to twenty-two million of my people, they wouldn't have to draft me. I'd join tomorrow. But I either have to obey the laws of the land or the laws of Allah. I have nothing to lose by standing up and following my beliefs. We've been in jail for four hundred years.

When choosing its top athletes of the twentieth century, the ESPN network placed Muhammad Ali at number three. The fighter was born Cassius Marcellus Clay, Jr., in Louisville, Kentucky. Taught to box at age twelve, he won 100 of 108 amateur fights and several national titles. At age eighteen, he added a gold medal from the 1960 Summer Olympics. Back home in Kentucky, when a restaurant refused to serve him because of his race, Clay took the Olympic medal from around his neck and threw it into the Ohio River.

The handsome and skillful Clay brought style and verbal wit to professional boxing. Both quick and powerful, he could "float like a butterfly and sting like a bee." In his twentieth match, fighting as the underdog, he became the world heavyweight champion. A surprised nation was further shocked when Clay announced shortly thereafter that he had joined the Nation of Islam and taken a Muslim name, Muhammad Ali.

By March 1967, his record stood at 29–0. One month later, he refused induction into the U.S. Army during the Vietnam War, claiming conscientious objector status. "I ain't got no quarrel with them Viet Cong," he said, adding, "No Viet Cong ever called me nigger." Condemned as unpatriotic and cowardly, Ali was stripped of his title and his boxing license. He was tried, found guilty, and sentenced to five years in prison. Released on appeal, he waited until 1971 for the U.S. Supreme Court to overturn the verdict.

Despite these years of inactivity, Ali ended his professional career with a record of fifty-six wins and five losses. Revered instead of scorned, he became the first boxer to win—and hold—the heavyweight championship three times (1964–1967, 1974–1978, and 1978–1979). But he stayed too long in the ring and lost three of his last four fights before retiring in 1981. Shortly after that, he was diagnosed with Parkinson's disease.

Ali was slowed by the disease but not defeated. Three decades after America reviled him for his religious and political beliefs, he was asked to light the Olympic torch at the opening of the 1996 Atlanta games. In his later years, Ali also worked alongside actor Michael J. Fox to raise awareness about and fund research on Parkinson's disease. In October 2003, the editor of *Esquire* magazine wrote that "he, like only a very few Americans, has existed for nearly his entire life at that rare nexus of celebrity, accomplishment, and infamy that makes one an American icon." Ali died in 2016, at the age of seventy-four.

If I thought going to war would bring freedom and equality to twenty-two million of my people, they wouldn't have to draft me. I'd join tomorrow. But I either have to obey the laws of the land or the laws of Allah. I have nothing to lose by standing up and following my beliefs. We've been in jail for four hundred years.

Muhammad Ali

Denise Altvatar

Activist, community organizer, cofounder of the Maine Wabanaki-State
Child Welfare Truth and Reconciliation Commission process; b. 1959

Having a place where my voice can be heard has changed my life dramatically, helping me to heal and giving me the strength to forgive. I still struggle to find a place in this world where I feel I belong. I believe I will find that place of belonging when I let people see who I really am, not only the truth of what has been done to me but what I have done to others. By acknowledging and sharing my truth, taking responsibility and seeking forgiveness, I can show my beautiful children, my family and my people that we can restore our hearts, minds and souls.

Denise's mother wasn't home when the Maine Department of Health and Human Services (DHHS) workers arrived at her house. They took seven-year-old Denise and her five sisters, threw the girls' clothes into garbage bags, packed them all into two station wagons, and drove away from the Passamaquoddy reservation at Pleasant Point. No one explained to them what was happening.

Denise and her sisters spent the next four years in a foster care nightmare. They were raped, starved, locked in a cold basement with rats overnight, made to stay in a urine-soaked bed for twenty-four hours at a time and to kneel on broom handles as punishment. When Denise and her sisters described their torture, social workers didn't believe them, and the punishments increased. Later, the sisters were split up, and although their day-to-day treatment improved, the trauma festered.

After being reunited with her mother seven years later, Denise continued to experience abuse on the reservation and suffered racist treatment at school. She was pregnant and married at sixteen.

Helped and encouraged by Sister Maureen, who ran the local school, Denise earned her high school diploma and enrolled at the University of Maine at Machias.

The American Friends Service Committee (AFSC) hired Denise in 1992 to create the AFSC Wabanaki Program, enabling her to serve the youth in her community in the ways that she had needed at their age: renewing cultural traditions, boosting social and job skills, and helping to deal with discrimination, domestic abuse, alcohol and drug addiction.

Denise has been a leading voice raising the alarm about the devastating impact of Oxycontin in Maine. And her work addressing racism in Maine's criminal justice system has earned her appointments to the Maine State Board of Visitors, the Maine Indian Tribal State Commission (MITSC), the Wabanaki Criminal Justice Commission (CJC), and the Department of Corrections Advisory Group.

When Maine was found to be out of compliance with the federal Indian Child Welfare Act (ICWA), Denise told her story for a training film about the experiences of Wabanaki people who had been in state foster care, and she helped train more than five hundred DHHS workers in Maine on the importance of ICWA. Denise's generous sharing made possible the historic work of the Maine Wabanaki-State Child Welfare Truth and Reconciliation Commission (TRC). The three goals of the TRC are: truth—acknowledge the truth about what happened to Wabanaki children and families involved with the Maine child welfare system; healing—create opportunities to heal and learn from the truth; and change—collaborate to operate the best child welfare system possible for Wabanaki children and families. The film *Dawnland* documents the TRC's historic work.

Having a place where my voice can be heard has changed my life dramatically helping me to heal and giving me the strength to forgive. I still struggle to find a place in this world where I feel I belong. I believe I will find that place of belonging when I let people see who I really am, not only the truth of what has been done to me but what I have done to others. By acknowledging and sharing my truth, taking responsibility and seeking forgiveness, I can show my beautiful children, my family and my people that we can restore our hearts, minds and souls.

Denise Altvater

Ella Baker

Civil rights organizer; b. 1903, d. 1986

In order for us as poor and oppressed people to become a part of a society that is meaningful, the system under which we now exist has to be radically changed. . . . It means facing a system that does not lend itself to your needs and devising means by which you can change that system. That is easier said than done.

The granddaughter of a slave who was beaten for refusing to marry a man her master chose for her, Ella Baker dedicated her life to working behind the scenes of the civil rights movement. If she could have changed anything about the movement, it might have been to persuade the men leading it that they, too, should do more work behind the scenes. Baker was a staunch believer in helping ordinary people to work together and lead themselves, and she objected to centralized authority. In her worldview, "strong people don't need strong leaders."

In 1927, after graduating from Shaw University, in Raleigh, North Carolina, Baker moved to Harlem and began her long organizing career by helping to establish consumer cooperatives during the Depression. She joined the NAACP's staff in 1938 and spent half of each year traveling in the South to build support for local branches, which would become the foundation of the civil rights movement. In 1946, she reduced her NAACP responsibilities to work on integrating New York City's public schools.

Baker was one of the visionaries who created the Southern Christian Leadership Conference (SCLC) in 1957, and she recruited the Reverend Martin Luther King, Jr., to serve in the organization. She served two terms as the SCLC's acting executive director but clashed with King, feeling that he controlled too much and empowered others too little.

In 1960, when four Black students in Greensboro, North Carolina, were refused service at a Woolworth's lunch counter, setting off sympathetic sit-ins across the country, Baker seized the day. Starting with student activists at her alma mater, she was instrumental in the founding of the nationwide Student Nonviolent Coordinating Committee (SNCC), which gave young Blacks, including women and the poor, a major role in the civil rights movement.

Baker returned to New York City in 1964 and worked for human rights until her death, in 1986. Her words live on in "Ella's Song," sung by Sweet Honey in the Rock: "We who believe in freedom cannot rest."

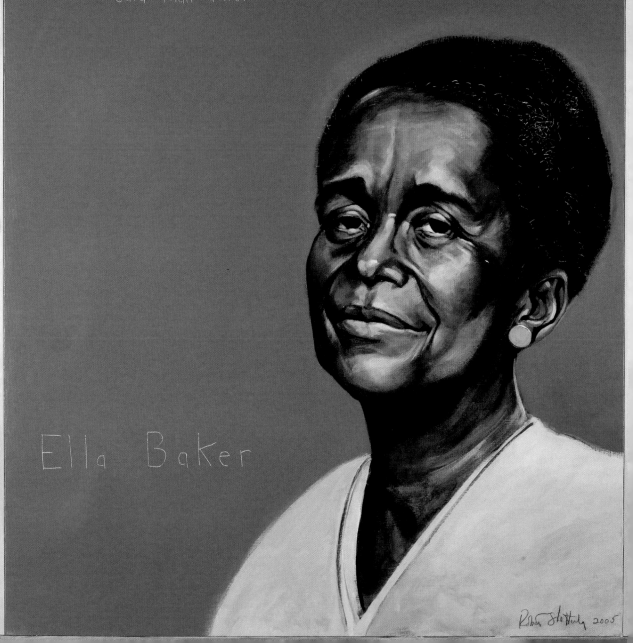

In order for us as poor and oppressed people to become a part of a society that is meaningful, the system under which we now exist has to be radically changed... It means facing a system that does not lend itself to your needs and devising means by which you change that system. That is easier said than done.

Ella Baker

Robert Shetterly 2005

James Baldwin

Novelist, essayist, playwright, poet, and social critic; b. 1924, d. 1987

People who shut their eyes to reality simply invite their own destruction, and anyone who insists on remaining in a state of innocence long after that innocence is dead turns himself into a monster.

Considered one of the greatest American writers of the twentieth century, James Baldwin was not only a novelist, essayist, playwright, and poet but also an activist, fearless in his effort to explore his personal struggles and the challenges facing a changing nation. He provided readers with powerful observations and critiques of a nation in the midst of a seismic social and cultural evolution.

Baldwin was born in New York City on August 2, 1924, to Emma Jones, who never told her son the identity of his father. His mother eventually married New York minister David Baldwin and gave her toddler her husband's last name. Though the relationship between stepfather and stepson was a tumultuous one, it didn't prevent Baldwin from following his stepfather into the church, where he served as a youth minister. Then at DeWitt Clinton High School, Baldwin nurtured his interest in words and writing, serving as literary editor for the school's magazine, where he also published his first writing.

Following his 1942 graduation from high school, Baldwin went to work to help his family make ends meet. A year later, his stepfather's untimely death increased Baldwin's responsibilities, but, while cycling through a series of jobs, Baldwin held on to his dream of making writing his career. Trips to New York's Greenwich Village, where he met many artistic and intellectual figures, fueled this desire, as did his mentors, painter Beauford Delaney and writer Richard Wright, who helped Baldwin secure his first writing fellowship.

In 1948, Baldwin traveled to Paris, France, on a fellowship. There, in a less racially inhibited culture, Baldwin felt the freedom to become the writer he wanted to be.

Baldwin published his first novel, the semi-autobiographical *Go Tell It on the Mountain*, in 1953, confronting his feelings about his faith and his relationship with his stepfather. Baldwin's play *The Amen Corner* (1954) shares the novel's themes of the Black church and family difficulties. Baldwin's now-classic collection of essays, *Notes of a Native Son* came out in 1955, and his second novel, *Giovanni's Room*, in 1956, in which he confronted his feelings about his homosexuality.

In 1957, Baldwin began writing magazine essays about race in America. Next came his books *Nobody Knows My Name: More Notes of a Native Son* (1961) and *The Fire Next Time* (1963)—among the most powerful works ever written about race and its devastating impact on the United States.

In 1965, Baldwin engaged in a famous debate with conservative William F. Buckley at England's Cambridge University. According to the host of the event, the Cambridge Union Society, Baldwin's pro–civil rights arguments convincingly defeated Buckley's counterarguments.

Baldwin participated in both the 1963 March on Washington and the march from Selma to Montgomery in 1965. Baldwin was devastated and exhausted by the assassinations of his friends Medgar Evers, Malcolm X, and Martin Luther King, Jr., and his personal fame begun to fade during the 1970s and 1980s, while his influence lived on in writers like Maya Angelou, Nikki Giovanni, and Toni Morrison.

Baldwin died at home in Saint-Paul-de-Vence, France, on December 1, 1987, and was buried at Ferncliff Cemetery in Hartsdale, New York.

People who shut their eyes to
reality simply invite their own
destruction, and anyone who insists
on remaining in a state of
innocence long after that
innocence is dead turns

himself into

a monster.

James Baldwin

Rev. Dr. William J. Barber II

Minister, organizer; b. 1963

Our concern is the moral fabric of our society. It's about a deep vision of society that says we must look at two guiding stars. The first is our state and national Constitutions, with their insistence on the common good, the good of the whole, and establishing equal justice under the law. And the second guiding star comes from the best of all our moral and ethical traditions, loving your neighbor and doing justice. It is from these two perspectives that public policy ought to be developed. We should ask, are policies constitutionally consistent, morally defensible, and economically sane.

"We have a new demographic emerging that is changing the South. The one thing they don't want to see is us crossing over racial lines and class lines and gender lines and labor lines. When this coalition comes together, you're going to see a New South." This vision of the New South reflects Rev. Dr. William J. Barber's upbringing in a family committed to inclusive change.

Born in Indianapolis, Indiana, on August 30, 1963 (two days after the March on Washington for Jobs and Freedom), Barber was five when his family moved back to his father's home of Washington County, North Carolina. Barber's father was the first African American teacher in the county's white high school, and his mother was the school's first African American office manager. Their desire to integrate and improve the broader community inspired Barber's activism. "I grew up under the tutelage of not understanding how to be a Christian without being concerned about justice and the larger community," he says.

Barber graduated from Washington County's Plymouth High School and matriculated at North Carolina Central University, a historically Black university in Durham. He earned a Master of Divinity degree from Duke University and a doctorate in Public Policy and Pastoral Care from Drew University. Barber married Rebecca McLean Barber; the couple has five children. For more than two decades, Barber has served as the pastor of the Greenleaf Christian Church (Disciples of Christ), in Goldsboro, North Carolina.

In response to the 2013 Republican takeover of the state legislature, followed by regressive legislation, Barber, president of the North Carolina chapter of the NAACP, launched the "Moral Mondays" movement. On February 8, 2014, thousands of protesters gathered at the "Mass Moral March" to show their support for the Moral Mondays movement and the principles it stands for. "Do not forget this is a movement, not a moment," Barber reminded the marchers as it brought atheists, Jews, Muslims, Christians, gays, straights, Republicans, Democrats, rich, poor, white, Black, Latinos, Asians, and others together to combat institutionalized privilege and racism. As a result of the attention garnered by North Carolina's Moral Mondays movement, other states, particularly southern states, have developed or are developing their own Fusion movements.

In 2017, Barber became coleader of the Poor People's Campaign: A National Call for Moral Revival. Barber's ability to simplify issues with his commanding moral authority and to build broad coalitions offers disparate progressive organizations throughout the United States a shared path toward fighting for common goals. Barber loves to get the crowd chanting "Forward together, not one step back!"

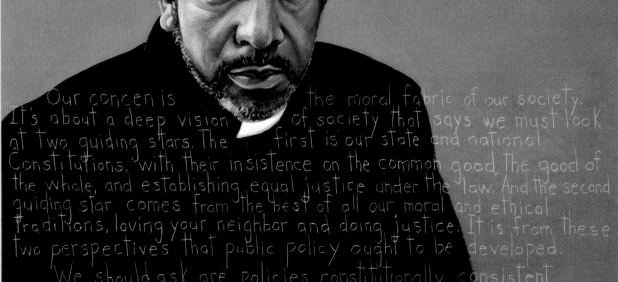

Rev. Dr. William J Barber II

Our concern is   the moral fabric of our society.
It's about a deep vision   of society that says we must look
at two guiding stars. The   first is our state and national
Constitutions, with their insistence on the common good. The good of
the whole, and establishing equal justice under the law. And the second
guiding star comes from the best of all our moral and ethical
traditions, loving your neighbor and doing justice. It is from these
two perspectives that public policy ought to be developed.
      We should ask, are policies constitutionally consistent,
morally defensible, and economically sane?

Robert Shetterly 2014

Anne Braden

Civil rights activist, writer; b. 1924, d. 2006

As long as people of color can be written off as expendable, and therefore acceptable victims of the most extreme inequities, none of the basic injustices of our society will be addressed; they will only get worse.

Anne Braden is best known for a single act: In 1954, she helped a Black couple buy a house in an all-white neighborhood of Louisville, Kentucky.

Anne and her husband were put on trial for sedition, blacklisted for jobs, threatened, and reviled by their fellow white southerners. But, as she said, "We never even thought of saying no. . . . We didn't really think about it [because] our minds were on other things."

The "other things" on Braden's mind had to do with gaining equal access, regardless of race, to nearly every other aspect of life in the South: hospitals, schools, parks, public transportation, restaurants, hotels, and more. "We lived in a segregated world," she explained, "but we were part of a community of black and white people who were opposing it."

Braden was an unlikely champion of racial equality. Born July 28, 1924, in Louisville but raised in the even more racially divided Anniston, Alabama, she was a member of the southern elite. Because her mother was descended from what was known as the "first settlers," Braden was raised to believe she was a member of a superior class of people. That idea started to bother her when she was still a girl.

While attending a church youth group to discuss "the Negro problem—which is what everybody called it if they talked about it at all," said Braden, "I made some mild comment that it seemed to me people ought to be treated equal no matter what color they were. And I can remember people looking a little startled and then somebody coming up to me later and saying, 'You shouldn't say things like that, people will think you're a communist.' "

Her first arrest—for protesting the execution of a Black man she believed to be wrongly convicted of rape—was in 1951. At the jail, she was threatened by a policeman. "[T]hat was a very revealing moment to me. All of my life police had been on my side. . . . All of a sudden I realized that I was on the other side. He had said, 'You're not a real southern woman.' And I said, 'No, I guess I'm not your kind of southern woman.' "

Her long career as an activist, beginning at age twenty, spanned six decades. Besides her efforts to end racism, she fought for workers' rights and helped organize labor unions. She opposed war, fought for amnesty for those who refused to go to war, and worked for nuclear disarmament. She championed women's rights and environmental justice. Braden was married to labor organizer Carl Braden and was a mother of three. She wrote a book about her sedition trial, *The Wall Between*, which was nominated for the National Book Award.

Anne Braden

As long as people of color can be written off as expendable, and therefore acceptable victims of the most extreme inequities, none of the basic injustices in our society will be addressed; they will only get worse.

Robert Shetterly 2012

John Brown

Tanner, sheep farmer, abolitionist, martyr; b. 1800, d. 1859

I, John Brown, am now quite certain that the crimes of this guilty land will never be purged away, but with Blood. I had, as I now think vainly, flattered myself that without very much bloodshed it might be done.

In July 1859, when pre–Civil War tensions between South and North were approaching a breaking point, twenty-one men, led by the militant abolitionist John Brown, raided and occupied the federal armory at Harper's Ferry, Virginia. Their plan was to distribute the armory's weapons to slaves throughout the region, forming a guerrilla force. From the cover of the Appalachian Mountains, the slaves would conduct raids against the South's slaveholders, free and arm still more slaves, and quickly destroy the South's "peculiar institution." Their plan failed; the U.S. Marines, led by Robert E. Lee, raided the reoccupied armory, killing ten of Brown's men and capturing seven more, including Brown.

This was not the first time Brown had resorted to violence. Back in 1855, Kansas was engulfed in a bloody struggle over whether the territory was to be admitted to the Union as a free or slave state. Brown moved to the territory and organized an informal paramilitary force intended to counter the bloodshed of the pro-slavery Border Ruffians. In 1856, amid increasing tensions, he and his men dragged five pro-slavery sympathizers from their homes in the middle of the night and hacked them to death with broadswords.

What are we to make of all this violence?

Not only was Brown one of the most committed abolitionists of his time—three of his sons would be killed fighting for their father's ideals—he was nearly alone in the equality and respect he showed African Americans, referring to them respectfully as "Mr." and "Mrs." and inviting them to share meals at the family table. He believed that slavery was such a moral abomination that nearly any violence was justified if it ended it. Frederick Douglass said this about John Brown: "His zeal in the cause of freedom was infinitely superior to mine. Mine was as the taper light; his was as the burning sun. Mine was bounded by time, his stretched away to the silent shores of eternity. I could speak for the slave. John Brown could fight for the slave. I could live for the slave. John Brown could die for the slave."

And Harriet Tubman said of Brown: "He done more in dying, than 100 men would in living."

John Brown was convicted of murder, treason, and conspiracy, and was hanged on December 2, 1859. Soon after, as Union soldiers marched south in the Civil War, they sang a new battle song, whose first verse ended with "John Brown's body lies a-mouldering in the grave/ His soul is marching on."

John Brown

I, John Brown, am now quite certain that the crimes of this guilty land will never be purged away, but with Blood. I had, as I now think vainly, flattered myself that without very much bloodshed it might be done.

Zyahna Bryant

Student activist, community organizer; b. 2001

*In the spring of 2016, I did something that scared me, but something that I knew needed to be done.
I wrote the petition, a letter to the editor and city council, calling for the removal of the Robert E.
Lee statue and the renaming of the park, formerly known as Robert E. Lee Park. I was 15.*

In the spring of 2016, fifteen-year-old high school student Zyahna Bryant, a Charlottesville native, drafted a petition for the removal of her city's statue of Confederate general Robert E. Lee. Her petition also called for renaming Lee Park, where the statue stood. In an interview, Bryant recalled: "[I]t wasn't until 5th or 6th grade, when we started learning about the Civil War that I started to really understand. . . . Once I learned the truth about slavery and the Civil War, I felt disgusted that my city wanted to display a statue that celebrated my ancestors' pain." A few years later, as a high school freshman, Bryant took to heart an assignment on "how to make a change," and the Robert E. Lee petition was born.

The petition proved to be a powerful catalyst, not only in her own community but across the country, for those who agreed with Bryant's goals. Though the city voted to remove the statute, Bryant's efforts faced many legal setbacks and counterprotests. In August 2017, white supremacists descended upon the city in an effort to preserve the statue, and antiracists rallied to counterprotest. Sadly, one person was murdered and several others injured when one of the white supremacists used his car as a weapon against a group of counterprotesters.

Meanwhile, the Lee Park has been renamed twice, first as Emancipation Park and then as Market Street Park; as of this writing, removal of the Lee statue is still tied up in a court challenge.

In a 2018 op-ed, Bryan explained that "[i]t has always been bigger than *just* a statue. There is truly a very long and intricate history of white supremacy that lurks beneath the bricks and sidewalks that the people of Charlottesville inhabit daily. . . . The debate over Confederate monuments in public spaces only mirrors the larger question of what community means, causing us to really reflect on the messages that we are transmitting about community through our public spaces."

When Bryant drafted her petition, she was already a seasoned organizer. In 2013, at the age of twelve, she had organized a protest to the verdict that freed the killer of Florida teenager Trayvon Martin. Later, Bryant founded her high school's Black Student Union and joined Black Lives Matter.

In 2018, Bryant was awarded the Student Stowe Prize by the Harriet Beecher Stowe Center, the Princeton Prize in Race Relations by Princeton University, and the Yale Basset Award for Community Engagement by Yale University. Bryant published her first book, *Reclaim: A Collection of Poetry and Essays,* in 2019, and was appointed to the Virginia African American Advisory Board by Governor Ralph Northam in the same year. Currently attending the University of Virginia, Bryant serves on the Council on UVA-Community Partnerships.

In the spring of 2016, I did something that scared me, but something that I knew needed to be done. I wrote the petition, a letter to the editor and city council, calling for the removal of the Robert E. Lee statue and the renaming of the park, formerly known as Robert E Lee Park, I was 15.

Zyahna Bryant

Robert Shetterly 2020

Tarana Burke

Activist for women's rights, nonprofit executive; b. 1973

Shame is debilitating. Empathy stamps out shame.
The Me Too Movement is about empowerment through empathy.

The #MeToo movement has become a focal point of the worldwide effort to address sexual violence. The movement is an outgrowth of activist Tarana Burke's phrase "me too," an expression which afforded her a way to make common cause with survivors of sexual violence. Burke explains that the phrase "me too" represents two sides of the same coin. "On one side, it's a bold declarative statement that 'I'm not ashamed,' and 'I'm not alone.' On the other side, it's a statement from survivor to survivor that says 'I see you, I hear you, I understand you and I'm here for you' or 'I get it.'"

Tarana Burke is a proud native of the Bronx. Burke's activism dates back to her adolescence and her involvement with the Selma-based 21st Century Youth Leadership Movement. Through that organization, Burke participated in her first organizing effort in support of five African American and Latino teenage boys who had been falsely accused of brutally sexually assaulting a jogger in New York City's Central Park.

Following high school, Burke attended Alabama State University and graduated from Auburn University, before moving to Selma to work for the 21st Century Youth Leadership Movement. During her time in Alabama, Burke founded the nonprofit Just Be Inc. (2006). She also encountered a girl—to whom she gave the pseudonym "Heaven"—whose story forced Burke to confront her own circumstance as a survivor of sexual violence, even though Burke couldn't yet bring herself to say "me too" out loud.

Recognizing the dearth of resources dedicated to helping young Black and brown girls, Burke and Just Be Inc. worked to support them: "to speak healing into their lives, to let them know that healing was possible, and let them know that they weren't alone." Meanwhile, Burke moved toward healing herself, which would make her a more effective leader. "When I learned to lean into my joy, my life changed."

Burke had been working to spread the "me too" message for more than a decade when, in 2017, her phrase was amplified in ways that no one could have predicted. Dozens of famous and powerful men were accused of sexual violence and sexual harassment. The Twitter hashtag #MeToo gave face to survivors of sexual violence, as well as let other survivors know they weren't alone. The call to solidarity around #MeToo was a resounding success as millions of people came out as survivors. Burke acknowledged the power of this catalytic moment, noting "what started as a simple exchange of empathy between survivors has now become a rallying cry, a movement builder and a clarion call. . . . With two words, folks who have been wearing the fear and shame that sexual violence leaves you with like a scarlet letter are able to come out into the sunlight and see that we are a global community."

Burke currently serves as a senior director with the Brooklyn-based nonprofit Girls for Gender Equity, and she is the mother of Kaia Burke.

Tarana Burke

Shame is debilitating. Empathy stomps out shame.
The Me Too Movement is about empowerment
through empathy.

Robert Shetterly 2018

Chief Joseph, Hinmatóowyalahtq'it

Native American leader; b. circa 1840, d. 1904

I have asked some of the great white chiefs where they get their authority to say to the Indian that he shall stay in one place, while he sees white men going where they please. They cannot tell me.

Son of a Nez Perce Indian chief, Joseph was born Hinmatóowyalahtq'it ("Thunder Rolling Down the Mountain") on land that is identified today as being in northeastern Oregon. He became known as Joseph the Younger because his father, one of the first Nez Perce to convert to Christianity, had taken Joseph as his baptismal name.

In 1863, following a gold rush, whose white participants entered the territory of the Nez Perce, the federal government claimed some six million acres of tribal land. Joseph the Elder renounced both the United States and Christianity. When he died, in 1871, his son became chief and soon had to deal with a very difficult choice.

When a U.S. general threatened a cavalry attack in 1877, Chief Joseph at first agreed to relocate his people, now diminished in size by 90 percent, to a reservation in Idaho. Before this could happen, however, a group of young Nez Perce warriors attacked white settlements along the Salmon River and then went to hide among the tribe. Joseph, who initially had believed that resistance to the U.S. military would be futile, was forced to resist. Moving north through the mountains of Idaho, Wyoming, and Montana, the Nez Perce, under his leadership, conducted one of the most brilliant retreats in American history. In a little more than three months, this band of seven hundred, with fewer than two hundred warriors, traveled almost fifteen hundred miles while fighting off a pursuing army of two thousand.

By the time the exhausted, starving Nez Perce were forced to surrender in early October 1877, just forty-two miles from the Canadian border, Joseph had become famous and was called "the Red Napoleon." In truth, his younger brother, Olikut, and others were the war leaders of their tribe, while Joseph was responsible for guarding the camp. Chief Joseph, however, is best remembered today for his elegant surrender speech, which has been called the most famous statement in Native American history. It ends, "Hear me, my chiefs; my heart is sick and sad. From where the sun now stands, I will fight no more forever."

Chief Joseph had been told that his people would be returned to their lands in Oregon, but, instead, they were transported to eastern Kansas, and then Oklahoma, where many died from epidemic diseases. He continued to protest their treatment, even traveling to Washington, D.C., in 1879 to meet with President Hayes, but he and the Nez Perce were never permitted to return to their homeland. He died in northeastern Washington State in 1904 and was buried there in exile.

Chief Joseph,
Hinmaton Yalaktit

I have asked some of the great
white chiefs where they get their
authority to say to the Indian
that he shall stay in one place,
while he sees white men going
where they please. They
can not tell me.

Shirley Chisholm

First Black congresswoman; b. 1924, d. 2005

. . . prejudice and hatred built the nation's slums, maintains them and profits by them. . . . Unless we start to fight and defeat the enemies in our own country, poverty and racism, and make our talk of equality and opportunity ring true, we are exposed in the eyes of the world as hypocrites when we talk about making people free.

"Fighting Shirley Chisholm—Unbought and Un-bossed" was her campaign slogan for New York's Twelfth Congressional District race in 1968. Chisholm won and then stayed true to her words throughout her political career. She opposed the Vietnam War and weapons development at a time when it was unpopular to do so and fought relentlessly for the rights of women, children, minorities, and people with low incomes.

Chisholm introduced groundbreaking legislation to establish publicly supported day-care centers and to expand unemployment insurance to cover domestic workers. She was a founding member of the Congressional Black Caucus, holding it accountable as "the conscience of Congress." In 1972, Chisholm announced her candidacy for the Democratic presidential nomination, the first African American woman to do so. Although she didn't receive the nomination, she won twenty-eight delegates and gathered 152 votes at the Democratic National Convention.

The daughter of immigrant parents from Barbados and Guyana, Chisholm grew up in Brooklyn, New York, where she remained passionately committed to her constituency. Before entering politics, she was a nursery school teacher, day-care center director, and a consultant for the New York Department of Social Services, where she became well acquainted with the struggles of the poor and disenfranchised. She chronicled her political career in two autobiographical books, *Unbought and Unbossed* (1970) and *The Good Fight* (1973).

Chisholm continued her advocacy after she retired from Congress in 1983, going on to cofound the National Political Congress of Black Women, to teach at Mount Holyoke College and Spelman College, and to lecture around the country. At every turn, she invited others to join her in fighting for a more just society. "We need men and women . . . who will dare to declare that they are free of the old ways that have led us wrong, and who owe nothing to the traditional concentrations of capital and power that have subverted this nation's ideals."

...prejudice and hatred built the nation's slums, maintains them and profits by them... Unless we start to fight and defeat the enemies in our own country, poverty and racism, and make our talk of equality and opportunity ring true, we are exposed in the eyes of the world as hypocrites when we talk about making people free.

Shirley Chisholm

Claudette Colvin

Civil rights activist; b. 1939

. . . as a teenager, I kept thinking, Why don't the adults around here just say something? Say it so that they know we don't accept segregation? I knew then and I know now that, when it comes to justice, there is no easy way to get it. You can't sugarcoat it. You have to take a stand and say, "This is not right." And I did.

Major movements in history are marked by big events but are always comprised of smaller events that are often overlooked. Claudette Colvin's story is one of these significant but overlooked events.

Her story begins as a young girl growing up in segregated Montgomery, Alabama. She knew firsthand of the humiliation and violence that Black people suffered if they did not toe the line of Jim Crow. Colvin, a studious child, was determined to get the best education possible, become a lawyer, and fight for civil rights.

On March 2, 1955, however, Colvin's life changed forever. The fifteen-year-old boarded a segregated city bus on her way home from school, her mind filled with what she'd been learning during Negro History Week. At one stop, several white passengers got on, and the bus driver ordered her and three others to move. Three got up; Colvin stayed. As she recalled, "I felt like Sojourner Truth was pushing down on one shoulder and Harriet Tubman was pushing down on the other—saying, 'Sit down girl!' I was glued to my seat."

She was taken off the bus by two police officers, whose behavior made her fear that she might be raped. She was charged with violating segregation laws, misconduct, and resisting arrest. Her conviction and subsequent probation left Colvin feeling she would never get the education and professional life she so desired.

The African American community was outraged. The Reverend Dr. Martin Luther King, Jr., came to Montgomery to fight her arrest, and leaders in the civil rights movement sought a way to end bus segregation. They looked at Claudette Colvin as a potential "face" of the movement. However, she was deemed too young and her complexion too dark to be the right fit.

Nine months later, Rosa Parks refused to give up her seat on a bus, and the boycott that was contemplated when Colvin was arrested began. Parks was educated, older, lighter-skinned, and employed as a seamstress. She had been trained for civil disobedience by the NAACP.

Claudette Colvin's role was not over. She and the three other young women who were harassed on that bus in 1955 became the plaintiffs in a lawsuit challenging the constitutionality of segregated buses. *Browder v. Gayle* went all the way to the Supreme Court, where the justices found that Montgomery's bus segregation was in violation of the Fourteenth Amendment, a significant civil rights victory.

Claudette Colvin: Twice Toward Justice, by Philip Hoose, winner of a National Book Award, tells her story.

as a teenager, I kept thinking, "Why don't the adults around here just say something? Say it so they know we don't accept segregation?" I knew then and I know now that, when it comes to justice, there is no easy way to get it. You can't sugarcoat it. You have to take a stand and say, "This is not right."
And I did.

Claudette
Colvin

Maulian Dana

Penobscot Nation Tribal Ambassador, human rights activist, poet; b. 1984

There is power in unity. When tribal nations are seen as sovereign bodies we can work together toward a better relationship with other governments. When cities and towns celebrate Indigenous People's Day, a foundation of trust and understanding can be created. When we are seen as people and not stereotypes or mascots, we can build on shared humanity. It is truly all about respect.

When Maulian Dana looks outside her home on the Penobscot Indian Island Reservation, she sees a place where, for centuries, her people have been connected. "I come from a long line of tribal leaders, and I was raised by strong women. . . . Both of my grandmothers had leadership positions in the tribe, and my father was Penobscot chief when I was a teenager. Seeing my dad's experiences as chief . . . helped shape who I am today."

In addition to her current role as the tribe's first officially recognized Penobscot Nation Tribal Ambassador, Dana serves on the board of the Maine Center for Economic Policy and on the Penobscot Nation Tribal Council. Previously, Dana served as the Human Resources director for Penobscot Indian Nation Enterprises and worked in the Penobscot Nation Cultural & Historic Preservation Department. She says, "I learned early on to speak my truth."

Dana recalls the uncomfortable feeling she had as a teenager as she watched a high school basketball game between the Nokomis Warriors and the Skowhegan Indians. The fans of both teams came to the game with painted faces—their idea of war paint— and wore Native American costumes, while making stereotypical war cries. Dana turned to her dad and said, "Is that how they think of us?" Dana saw in that moment that the use of Native Americans as mascots must end. She explained that "these displays incite dangerous thought patterns that lead to racist and sometimes violent behavior against the marginalized target group."

In high school, Dana joined in the effort to help educate communities about the harm that stereotyping Native Americans as mascots brings to both Native American and non–Native American communities. She continued her efforts at the University of Maine, Orono, where she received the prestigious Margaret Chase Smith Public Affairs Scholarship in 2005 and graduated in 2006 with a degree in political science. In 2007, Dana published a book of poetry, *Through These Eyes: Poetry of a Penobscot Woman.*

From her moment of rage as a teenager to her appointment as ambassador of her people's nation, her work has made a big impact; more than twenty schools in Maine stopped using Native American–related mascots.

Through her role as ambassador, Dana advocates her people's positions on issues ranging from land use, water rights, and tribal sovereignty to violence against Native American women. During her first year in that position, Dana realized two of her longtime goals. The Maine legislature voted in 2019 to ban the use of Native American mascots in public schools. And on April 26, 2019, Governor Janet Mills signed legislation that replaces Columbus Day with Indigenous Peoples' Day, joining a handful of other states. There is no question that Dana's early start at "speaking her truth" is transforming the perception of Native peoples in the state of Maine.

Maulian Dana

There is power in unity. When tribal nations are seen as sovereign bodies we can work towards a better relationship with other governments. When cities and towns celebrate Indigenous People's Day, a foundation of trust and understanding can be created. When we are seen as people and not stereotypes or mascots, we can build on shared humanity. It is truly all about respect.

Robert Shetterly 2019

Deqa Dhalac

Community activist and organizer; b. 1966

As a black, immigrant, Muslim woman, I want to be a force for positive change in my community, to use my voice to advocate for the changes my community wishes to see—an end to racism, better housing and jobs, better schools, cleaner environment, where everyone feels welcomed and included, where we embrace and celebrate diverse cultures.

Activist and community organizer Deqa Dhalac teaches us to lead from the collective wisdom of the community. This leadership style is rooted in her native Somali culture and the deep, rich soil of her life experience.

From a young age, Dhalac was influenced by her pro-democracy activist father who participated in a coup before she was born and later was jailed many times for speaking out against a corrupt, dictatorial government. Among many female role models, Dhalac singles out her mother, who could not read or write in her own language and had never been to school but was multitalented. Growing up in Mogadishu amid a lively extended family, Dhalac received private language instruction (English, Italian, and Arabic). Later, she earned an accounting degree. As an immigrant to the United States, she appreciates her advantage, avoiding the "language barriers many of my community members struggle with."

Dhalac's path to American citizenship was a circuitous one. Like many politically active Somalis, her parents focused on getting their children out of the war-torn country to safety. When Dhalac left Somalia, she first traveled to Italy, then to England and Canada, before settling in Atlanta in 1992, where her three children were born. While working for hotels in Atlanta, Dhalac met other Somali immigrants and began community organizing around voting rights.

Dhalac decided to relocate her family to Lewiston, Maine, where her uncle lived. Lewiston was a smaller and friendlier place, with a large number of Somali immigrants who were already business owners and community leaders. Before she knew it, Deqa was acting as an interpreter for Catholic Charities, then began working part-time for the city of Portland, helping people who were arriving from refugee camps.

Dhalac took on numerous nonprofit community-building positions and returned to school to hone her skills, earning two master's degrees, one in development policy and one in social work.

Currently working at the Maine Department of Education, Dhalac's priority projects include introducing schools to a new social-emotional learning curriculum, offering cultural responsiveness training for teachers, and bringing restorative justice into the educational setting.

In 2018, members of her community drafted Dhalac to run in a special election for South Portland's District 5 City Council seat. Running on a platform of representing all people, prioritizing affordable housing, environmental protection, and public education, she won the election by a comfortable margin. She also made local history as the first African American and first Muslim to be elected to the South Portland City Council.

For Dhalac, sound leadership requires listening and empathy—and taking her lead from collective community wisdom. "In my culture, if I don't have the answer, I won't pretend that I do. You ask your brothers and sisters to help you solve problems."

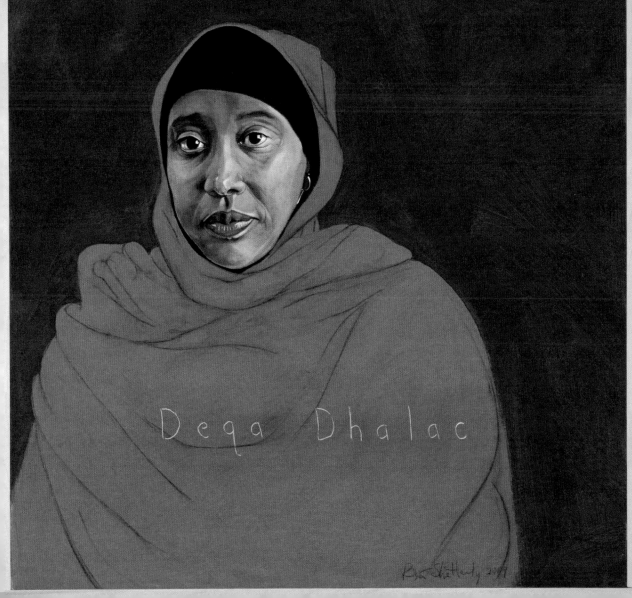

As a black, immigrant, Muslim woman, I want to be a force for positive change in my community, to use my voice to advocate for the changes my community members wish to see — an end to racism, better housing and jobs, better schools, cleaner environment, where everyone feels welcomed and included, where we embrace and celebrate our diverse cultures.

Deqa Dhalac

Frederick Douglass

Antislavery orator, writer; b. 1818, d. 1895

Where justice is denied, where poverty is enforced, where ignorance prevails, and where any one class is made to feel that society is an organized conspiracy to oppress, rob, and degrade them, neither persons nor property will be safe.

Born into slavery on the eastern shore of Maryland, Frederick Douglass was sent at age ten to labor for a family in Baltimore, where his slave master's sympathetic wife taught him the rudiments of reading and writing. With no formal schooling, Douglass educated himself by reading everything he could get his hands on. (He took his last name from the hero of Sir Walter Scott's epic poem *The Lady of the Lake.*) In his late teens, he was hired out to a cruel master, whom he defied in an act of great moral and physical courage. Disguised as a sailor, the twenty-year-old Douglass escaped to New York and began his extraordinary career as an abolitionist orator, writer, newspaper publisher, and governmental official.

Douglass published three autobiographical books. The first and most influential of these is *Narrative of the Life of Frederick Douglass, an American Slave, Written by Himself* (1845). The book focuses on the victims of slavery and the barbaric crimes inflicted upon them. It was an immediate success and today is considered a classic slave narrative.

A powerful physical presence and a superb orator, Douglass dramatically preached freedom and independence for slaves. His speech "What to the Slave is the Fourth of July?" may be the greatest statement ever of the moral and physical harm of slavery, while exposing the hypocrisy of white people for their founding ideals.

He was also an early champion of women's rights, printing the motto "Right Is Of No Sex—Truth Is Of No Color" on the masthead of his abolitionist newspaper *The North Star.* His vision became international in scope; he advocated fair treatment for working people in England, Ireland, and Scotland. Yet his most significant work continued to be in the United States.

During the Civil War, Douglass wrote, "We are fighting for unity; unity of idea, unity of sentiment, unity of object, unity of institutions, in which there shall be no North, no South, no East, no West, no black, no white, but a solidarity of the nation, making every slave free, and every free man a voter."

Frederick
Douglass

Where justice is denied, where poverty is enforced, where ignorance prevails, and where any one class is made to feel that society is in an organized conspiracy to oppress, rob, and degrade them, neither persons nor property will be safe.

W. E. B. Du Bois

Writer, teacher, civil rights spokesman; b. 1868, d. 1963

. . . back of the problem of race and color lies a greater problem . . . and that is the fact so many civilized persons are willing to live in comfort even if the price of this is poverty, ignorance and disease of the majority of their fellowmen, that to maintain this privilege men have waged war until today war tends to become universal and continuous . . .

William Edward Burghardt Du Bois is considered by many to be the father of African American studies. As a professor, historian, civil rights activist, and editor, Du Bois used his prodigious intellect to advance the cause of African American equality within the United States, as well as to advocate for Pan-African collaboration.

Born in Great Barrington, Massachusetts, on February 23, 1868, Du Bois grew up in an integrated community, received a quality education, and was praised for his intellectual gifts. Following his graduation from the local high school (where he was the school's first African American graduate), Du Bois attended Fisk University, in Nashville, Tennessee—Du Bois's first encounter with the American South.

Following Du Bois's 1888 graduation from Fisk, he entered Harvard University as a junior. By 1895, Du Bois had completed his bachelor's, master's, and doctoral degrees (the first African American to earn a Ph.D. from Harvard).

In 1896, Du Bois accepted a one-year research appointment at the University of Pennsylvania, where he started what would become his monumental study *The Philadelphia Negro* (1899), the first sociological study of an African American community.

Du Bois published his most important academic works while teaching at Atlanta University, including *The Souls of Black Folk* (1903) and *Black Reconstruction in America* (1935).

Du Bois was a cofounder of the Niagara Movement, a civil rights group established in 1905, which led to the 1909 creation of the National Association for the Advancement of Colored People (NAACP), where Du Bois served as a board member and as editor of the organization's magazine, *The Crisis*. This gave Du Bois a prominent platform for voicing his opinions about the labor movement and women's rights, lending early support to Harlem Renaissance artists, and advocating for Pan-Africanism and African self-determination.

Du Bois was investigated by the U.S. government following World War II for his critique of capitalism's role in sustaining poverty within the African American community and for his associations with people, such as actor/activist Paul Robeson, who were sympathetic to communism. Du Bois refused to discontinue his associations with people whose politics the U.S. government deemed undesirable.

In 1961, at the invitation of Kwame Nkrumah, president of the newly independent nation of Ghana, Du Bois embarked on a new project, an *Encyclopedia Africana*. Du Bois moved to Accra, Ghana, renounced his U.S. citizenship, and remained there until his death, at ninety-five, on August 27, 1963.

Du Bois's death was announced the next day at the March on Washington. Many people hoped, as Du Bois had long claimed, that America would finally understand that "the cost of liberty is less than the price of repression." DuBois also said, "Either the United States will destroy ignorance or ignorance will destroy the United States."

W. E. B. Du Bois

... back of the problem of race and color, lies a greater problem ... and that is the fact so many civilized persons are willing to live in comfort even if the price of this is poverty, ignorance and disease of the majority of their fellowmen, that to maintain this privilege men have waged war until today war tends to become universal and continuous ...

Alicia Garza

Human rights advocate; b. 1981

Power means making decisions over your own life, determining where resources go and don't go. Power is shaping the narrative of what is right, wrong, just, and unjust. Power is consequences when the people you elect don't carry out the agenda that you elected them to. Black people deserve to be powerful. Time and time again we have challenged this country to live up to its values of freedom, justice, democracy for all.

In the wake of the July 2013 murder of Florida teenager Trayvon Martin, Alicia Garza reacted on Facebook, using the phrase "Black lives matter." Little did she know then that these words would launch a movement. Patrisse Cullors turned those words into a hashtag that went viral. Opal Tometi harnessed the mounting energy around these words by designing social media platforms and connecting activists interested in transforming #BlackLivesMatter into a political force.

The underlying concerns of the Black Lives Matter movement were not new, but its formulation as an international, decentralized social justice movement of the digital age, established by three women of color, has been revolutionary. "Wherever you feel you can make the greatest contribution, you should," says Garza. "We are ordinary people attempting to do extraordinary things. . . ."

Garza, who grew up as Alicia Schwarz in a mixed-race, mixed-religion household in Marin County, came out as queer when she was twenty-three. Garza met her husband, Malachi Garza, a transgender male changemaker, through activist training the year after her college graduation from the University of California, San Diego. They married in 2008.

Garza is "driven by wanting to see change in my lifetime." In addition to cofounding Black Lives Matter, Garza has served as executive director of People Organized to Win Employment Rights (POWER), board chair of the Right to the City Alliance (RTTC), and board member of the School of Unity and Liberation (SOUL), which trains young community-based social justice activists. Garza is also the Strategy and Partnerships director for the National Domestic Workers Alliance.

In 2018, Garza established the Black Futures Lab, a project focused on identifying ways to engage African Americans in meaningful grassroots change.

Garza is also cofounder (with Ai-jen Poo and Cecile Richards) of Supermajority, an organization dedicated to advancing equity for women through advocacy, electoral politics, and community organizing. In a June 2019 speech, Garza explained, "Supermajority says that it will be women, cisgender and trans, that will shape what happens. . . . With Supermajority, we are saying that we are forming a wall of women. And you will have to get through women to accomplish anything at all in this country."

Always bringing a sense of urgency to her work, Garza acknowledges the longer struggle: "[W]hat I've learned from some of the people that have survived [the civil rights era] is that we have to be in it for the long haul. . . . [W]e should be preparing ourselves for a long fight."

Alicia Garza

Power means making decisions over your own life, determining where resources go and don't go. Power is shaping the narrative of what is right, wrong, just, and unjust. Power is consequences when the people you elect don't carry out the agenda that you elected them to. Black people deserve to be powerful. Time and time again we have challenged this country to live up to its values of freedom, justice, democracy for all.

RW Shetterly 2019

Fannie Lou Hamer

Sharecropper, civil rights activist; b. 1917, d. 1977

*Sometimes it seem like to tell the truth today is to run the risk of being killed. But if I fall,
I'll fall five feet four inches forward in the fight for freedom. I'm not backing off.*

Fannie Lou Hamer, a Mississippi sharecropper, changed this nation's perspective on democracy. She worked for political, social, and economic equality for herself and all African Americans. She fought to integrate the national Democratic Party and became one of the first Black delegates to a presidential nominating convention.

Fannie Lou Townsend was born in Montgomery County, Mississippi, in 1917, the youngest of twenty children. By the age of six, she was working in the cotton fields. Although she dropped out of school at age twelve, she continued her education with Bible study. When she was twelve, her parents accumulated enough money to rent a farm and buy mules and tools for farming. A white neighbor poisoned their mules, forcing them into even greater debt. On the plantation where she worked, Fannie Lou met her future husband, Perry Hamer. Her Christian faith was a source of strength for her throughout her life, and she became known in the civil rights movement as a captivating preacher and singer, inspiring others with her moral and physical courage.

In 1962, the Student Nonviolence Coordinating Committee (SNCC) came to Hamer's town and encouraged African Americans to register as voters. Hamer volunteered, even though she had not previously known that voting was a constitutional right. After registering herself and working with SNCC, she lost her job, received death threats, and was severely beaten by the police in an effort to intimidate her. Hamer helped found the Mississippi Freedom Democratic Party (MFDP) in 1964 because African Americans were not allowed in the all-white Democratic Party delegation. Although Lyndon Johnson refused to seat the MFDP, the Democrats agreed that in the future no delegation would be seated from a state where anyone was illegally denied the right to vote.

Hamer also worked toward achieving financial independence for African Americans. In 1969, she helped to start the Freedom Farm Cooperative, which lent land to African Americans until they had enough money to buy it. She worked with the National Council of Negro Women, organized food cooperatives, and helped convene the National Women's Political Caucus in 1971.

Though Hamer wanted children, a white doctor had sterilized her without permission, so she adopted daughters instead. In her last years, she received many honors and awards. Engraved on her headstone in her hometown of Ruleville, Mississippi, are her famous words: "I'm sick and tired of being sick and tired."

Sometimes it seem like to tell the truth today is to run the risk of being killed. But if I fall, I'll fall five feet four inches forward in the fight for freedom. I'm not backing off.

Fannie Lou Hamer

Charles Hamilton Houston

Lawyer, architect of the civil rights legal strategy; b. 1895, d. 1950

*Lawsuits mean little unless supported by public opinion. Nobody needs to explain to
a Negro the difference between the law in the books and the law in action. . . .
The really baffling problem is how to create the proper kind of public opinion.*

"A lawyer's either a social engineer or he's a parasite on society," wrote Charles Hamilton Houston. Although trained as an attorney, he proved to be a formidable social engineer, establishing the strategy that ultimately took down the legal foundations of segregation in the United States, particularly in the field of education.

Houston was the grandson of Thomas Jefferson Houston, who escaped from slavery, then became a minister and an Underground Railroad conductor. His father was an attorney; his mother, a former teacher. Born in 1895, Houston attended Paul Laurence Dunbar High School in Washington, D.C., went on to Amherst College, where he was the only African American student in his class, then completed his LL.B. in 1922, and his S.J.D. (doctor of juridical science) at Harvard in 1923. Houston was both the first African American elected to the editorial board of the *Harvard Law Review* and the first African American to earn an S.J.D. at the university.

In the time between Amherst and Harvard, Houston served as a judge advocate during World War I— a member of the first class of African American men trained as U.S. Army officers. Houston was nearly lynched in France by white American soldiers because they didn't like seeing an African American officer interacting with a white French woman. "The hate and scorn showered on us Negro officers by our fellow Americans convinced me that there was no sense in my dying for a world ruled by them. I made up my mind that if I got through this war I would study law and use my time fighting for men who could not strike back."

Houston kept his word. In 1924, he joined his father's law practice in Washington, D.C. He also served as an administrator and a professor at Howard University's relatively new law school, training a large number of African American attorneys, including the future legal luminaries Thurgood Marshall and Oliver Hill, and crafting legal arguments to dismantle legalized segregation.

In 1935, Houston began serving as legal counsel for the NAACP, where he could test his legal strategies. The end goal was to overturn the infamous *Plessy v. Ferguson* decision of 1896, which enshrined the constitutional doctrine of "separate but equal." In 1938, Houston won the case of *Missouri ex rel. Gaines v. Canada*, securing African American plaintiff Gaines's admission to the all-white University of Missouri law school.

After leaving the NAACP in 1940, Houston continued to work on cases that attacked the "separate but equal" doctrine. With each victory, he and his colleagues weakened segregation's legal foundation, also winning cases involving union representation and discriminatory housing covenants.

Houston died of a heart attack in 1950, at age fifty-four. But his students—Marshall, Hill, and others—continued to expand the campaign that their teacher had begun, heeding his words: "There is no such thing as 'separate but equal.' Segregation itself imports inequality."

Charles Hamilton Houston

Robert Shetterly 2014

Law suits mean   little unless supported
by public opinion. Nobody   needs to explain to a Negro
the difference between   the law in the books and the
law in action...
                    The really baffling problem is how to
create the proper kind of public opinion.

Langston Hughes

Poet, novelist, playwright; b. 1902, d. 1967

Out of the rack and ruin of our gangster death,/ The rape and rot of graft, and stealth, and lies,/
We, the people, must redeem/ The land, the mines, the plants, the rivers./ The mountains and
the endless plain—/ All, all the stretch of these great green states—/ And make America again!

The words of "Let America Be America Again" are as alive and relevant today as they were when Langston Hughes wrote them in 1935. They remind us that we, the people, are responsible for our government and our future.

Hughes's words have inspired—and challenged—millions of people since he published his first volume of poetry, *The Weary Blues,* in 1926. He was among the first to write about the African American experience in language that reflected and celebrated the culture. Born in Joplin, Missouri, to mixed-race parents who divorced when he was young, Hughes was raised mostly by his maternal grandmother, Mary Patterson Langston. Her first husband, Lewis Leary, was an abolitionist who died at Harper's Ferry as a member of John Brown's band. Inspired by Mary to write about African Americans, Hughes wrote his first poem when he was thirteen.

Hughes attended Columbia University for a year and then traveled to Africa and Europe, working as a seaman. He continued to write, and by the time he returned to the United States in 1924, he had gained a reputation in African American literary circles as a gifted young poet. His work was central to the Harlem Renaissance of the 1920s. Among his innovations was the fusion of traditional verse with jazz and blues.

In the early 1930s, after he visited the then Soviet Union, Hughes's work took a more political turn. He spent the rest of the decade writing plays and poems that blended socialist messages, Black Nationalism, and the blues.

Throughout his life, Hughes remained convinced that art should be made accessible to as many people as possible. He made a monumental contribution to this effort with ten volumes of poetry, eight short story collections, two novels, a number of children's books, a two-volume autobiography, and many plays, essays, and translations. With his powerful words, Hughes celebrated Black culture and music and a universal humanity.

Langston Hughes

Out of the rack and ruin of our gangster death,
The rape and rot of graft, and stealth, and lies,
We, the people, must redeem
The land, the mines, the plants, the rivers.
The mountains and the endless plain —
All, all the stretch of these great green states —
And make America again!

K.A.S Shetterly 2005

Regina Jackson

Community builder; b. 1962.

Our children navigate trauma-filled streets and homes and suffer from complex PTSD as a result—
yes, PTSD is not just for soldiers who return home from war. Our kids don't get to leave their
battlefield. We need a revolution—a revolution of tenderness, a revolution of kindness—
where compassion and empathy are not nice to have. They are required.

Character, readiness, and access. Focusing on these three touchstones, Regina Jackson, the president and CEO of the East Oakland Youth Development Center (EOYDC), prepares some of the nation's most at-risk youth for positive professional and personal lives and social leadership roles.

Jackson was raised in Oakland and graduated in 1984 from the University of California, Berkeley. Following graduation, Jackson participated in the Coro Foundation's Fellowship in Public Affairs, which, in turn, led her to serve on the board of the EOYDC, a community-based, corporate-funded organization founded in 1978. Thirty-some years later, it is clear that EOYDC and Jackson are a great fit. "Service was very important to me, and I've been a cheerleader all of my life. So I'm happy to cheer here [at EOYDC] for the development and future molding and shaping of Oakland's young."

EOYDC hired Jackson to serve as its president and CEO in 1994, when the organization was over budget and lacked focus. Jackson completed a full reorganization, streamlining EOYDC's programs and securing its long-term fiscal health. She brought in new partners, including the Hewlett Foundation, the Oakland A's, and the Golden State Warriors.

As part of the restructuring, Jackson implemented her three-pillared "theory of change" model: 1. character building; 2. readiness (for future opportunities); 3. access (to higher education and/or professions that may interest young people). "Leading is not about when things are going great. True leaders show up when things are falling apart, and those pillars [character, readiness and access] . . . will see [young people] through."

Under Jackson's leadership, EOYDC has also worked to become a safe harbor and center of excellence. Located in a section of Oakland that has been called the "Killer Corridor," "...[t]here needed to be a beacon of hope, a north star, a safe place where you can go and get away from some of the negatives of the community. You can come here and be empowered, encouraged and valued. . . . Because my staff and I believe our youth can perform at high levels, they often rise to meet and exceed those expectations."

Jackson's methods have made a difference. High percentages of EOYDC youth go on to college and graduate school, the military, and directly into full-time work. Jackson has led by example, continuing with her education through certification programs and fellowships.

For some youth, traveling outside of Oakland and the San Francisco Bay Area will be a first-time experience. Such trips include college visits and cultural tours. Through two Obama administration initiatives (My Brother's Keeper and 100,000 Strong), Jackson led delegations of EOYDC students to China.

According to Jackson, "There's nothing more exciting and enriching to see that each and every day you're having an impact on a child's life. And that's what keeps me here."

Our children navigate trauma-filled streets and homes and
suffer from complex PTSD as a result – yes, PTSD is not just
for soldiers who return home from war. Our Kids don't get
to leave their battlefield. We need a revolution – a revolution
of tenderness, a revolution of Kindness – where compassion and
empathy are not nice to have, they are required!

Regina Jackson

Barbara Johns

Civil rights activist; b. 1935, d. 1991

*It was time that Negroes were treated equally with whites, time that they had
a decent school, time for the students themselves to do something about it. . . .
There wasn't any fear. I just thought—this is your moment. Seize it!*

Sometimes a courageous act by one person can set in motion a series of events that bring justice to an entire nation. Barbara Rose Johns has such a story to tell.

Johns was born in 1935 to Violet and Robert Johns of New York City. During World War II, she moved to Farmville, in Prince Edward County, Virginia, to live with her maternal grandmother, Mary Croner. She spent most of her youth living and working on her grandmother's farm, then later on her father's farm.

After years of frustration with the segregated Prince Edward County schools—which she described in a memoir as having poor facilities, shabby equipment, and no science laboratories or gymnasium—Barbara voiced her complaints to a teacher, who responded by asking her to "do something about it." Believing that her teacher's comments were dismissive of her concerns, she felt discouraged. However, after months of contemplation, she began to formulate a plan.

As Barbara described it, "The plan I felt was divinely inspired because I hadn't been able to think of anything until then. The plan was to assemble together the student council members. . . . From this, we would formulate plans to go on strike. We would make signs and I would give a speech stating our dissatisfaction and we would march out [of] the school and people would hear us and see us and understand our difficulty and would sympathize with our plight and would grant us our new school building and our teachers would be proud and the students would learn more and it would be grand."

Seizing the moment on April 23, 1951, Barbara Johns—by then a sixteen-year-old high school student—led her classmates to strike in protest of the substandard conditions at Robert Russa Moton High School. Her idealism, planning, and persistence ultimately garnered the support of NAACP lawyers Spottswood Robinson and Oliver Hill, who took up her cause of creating more equitable conditions for Moton High School.

After meeting with the students and the community, lawyers Robinson and Hill filed their case, *Davis v. Prince Edward,* at the federal courthouse in Richmond, Virginia. In 1954, the Farmville case became one of five cases that the U.S. Supreme Court reviewed in *Brown v. Board of Education of Topeka,* the landmark ruling that school segregation is unconstitutional.

After the strike, followed by reactionary threats from local racist groups, Barbara's family became concerned for her safety. They sent Barbara to Montgomery, Alabama, to finish her schooling. After graduating from high school, she attended Spelman College, in Atlanta, Georgia, and ultimately graduated from Drexel University in Philadelphia, Pennsylvania. Barbara Johns went on to lead a quiet life; she married the Reverend William Powell, raised five children, and was a librarian in the Philadelphia Public Schools. Barbara Johns Powell died in 1991.

Note: Thanks to the Moton Museum for contributing the original version of this biographical summary.

Barbara Johns

It was time that Negroes were treated equally with whites, time that they had a decent school, time for the students themselves to do something about it.

There wasn't any fear. I just felt — this is your moment. Seize it!

Robin Shetterly 2010

Clyde Kennard

Veteran, student, civil rights activist; b. 1927, d. 1963

What happened to me isn't as bad as what happened to the guard [the prison guard who abused me],
because this system has turned him into a beast, and it will turn his children into beasts.

There are two Clyde Kennard histories. The first is the story of Kennard's persistent struggle to enroll in the all-white Mississippi Southern College. To pay for his audacity, Kennard was framed on a false robbery charge and sent to prison for most of his remaining years. The second story is about the people who refused to let this injustice stand uncorrected.

Clyde Kennard was born in 1927 in Hattiesburg, Mississippi. At age twelve, he followed an older sister north to Chicago to go to school. When he turned eighteen, he joined the military and served for seven years, first in Germany after World War II and then in the Korean War. After receiving an honorable discharge, he enrolled at the University of Chicago. Three years into a political science degree program, Kennard was called to help his mother run the family farm after his stepfather's death. Back in Mississippi, hoping to complete his college degree, Kennard decided to apply to the nearby all-white college (now the University of Southern Mississippi).

Kennard applied three times, in 1955, 1958, and 1959, but was met with one racist barrier after another. In September 1960, after years of his escalating public fight to attend the college, Kennard was framed for allegedly masterminding the heist of twenty-five dollars' worth of chicken feed. Convicted by an all-white jury, he was sentenced to seven years hard labor at Parchman Penitentiary—one year for each $3.57 of feed.

The racist abuses continued in prison. After developing cancer, Kennard was refused treatment, and forced to continue working in the fields. He was released only after Medgar Evers, Martin Luther King, Jr., and others pressured the state. By then, he was too ill to recover.

After his death, on July 4, 1963, Kennard's story survived as little more than a footnote to the primary narratives of the civil rights movement.

Almost thirty years later, the Jackson, Mississippi, *Clarion-Ledger* published previously secret official documents showing that Kennard had been framed. After another fourteen years, Jerry Mitchell, an investigative reporter, interviewed the key witness against Kennard, establishing that Kennard's desire to attend college was his only crime.

Kennard's case came to the attention of a high school teacher in Chicago. He and his students teamed up with other advocates, including Steve Drizin, director of the Center on Wrongful Convictions at Northwestern University's Pritzker School of Law, to clear Kennard's name.

Finally, on May 16, 2006, the case was heard in the same court where the thirty-three-year-old Kennard had been convicted. The presiding judge, Robert Helfrich, declared Kennard's innocence. Steve Drizin called it "one of the saddest [cases] of the civil rights era because [Kennard] was silenced by 'respectable' people—academics, politicians, lawyers, prosecutors, judges, businessmen—all acting under the 'color of law.'"

On the day of his exoneration Clyde Kennard would have been nearly seventy-nine years old.

Clyde Kennard

What happened to me isn't as bad as what happened to the guard [the prison guard who abused me], because this system has turned him into a beast, and it will turn his children into beasts.

Martin Luther King, Jr.

Clergyman, civil rights leader; b. 1929, d. 1968

Nonviolence is a powerful and just weapon . . . which cuts without wounding and ennobles the man who wields it. It is a sword that heals.

Martin Luther King, Jr., was born in Atlanta, Georgia, the son of a Baptist minister. He completed his formal education with degrees from Morehouse College, Crozier Theological Seminary, and Boston University (Ph.D. in systematic theology, 1955). While serving as pastor of the Dexter Avenue Baptist Church in Montgomery, Alabama, King led the boycott that resulted in the desegregation of that city's bus system. Along with Ralph Abernathy, Ella Baker, and others, he went on to organize the Southern Christian Leadership Conference (SCLC)—commonly described as a group created to harness the moral authority and organizing power of Black churches to conduct nonviolent protest in the service of civil rights. King led SCLC until his death. His resolve in the face of threats to his safety, as well as that of his family, his conviction that "injustice anywhere is a threat to justice everywhere," and his ability to write and speak with extraordinary power and clarity brought him to national prominence as a leader of the movement to achieve racial justice in America.

King studied the writings and example of Mohandas K. Gandhi in India, who powerfully influenced his philosophy of nonviolence. When he accepted the Nobel Peace Prize in 1964, King said, "Nonviolence is not sterile passivity, but a powerful moral force which makes for social transformation." Like Gandhi, King also understood the strategic value of nonviolence: "We have neither the techniques nor the numbers to win a violent campaign." His commitment to nonviolence led him, over the objections of many people in the civil rights movement, to oppose the war in Vietnam; he understood the connections between racism, militarism, and materialism.

Like Henry David Thoreau, Dr. King believed in the necessity of resisting unjust laws with civil disobedience. As a leader of many demonstrations in support of the rights of African Americans, he was subject to frequent arrest and imprisonment. His "Letter from Birmingham Jail" (1963) was a call to conscience directed primarily at American religious leaders.

When a fellow civil rights worker was killed after the 1965 march from Selma to Montgomery, Alabama, King said: "If physical death is the price that some must pay to free their children and their white brothers from an eternal psychological death, then nothing can be more redemptive." Martin Luther King's own redemptive sacrifice was exacted by an assassin's bullet on April 4, 1968, in Memphis, Tennessee.

Martin Luther King. Jr

Nonviolence is a powerful
and just weapon... which cuts
without wounding and ennobles
the man who wields it. It is a
sword that heals

John Lewis

Civil rights activist, congressman; b. 1940, d. 2020

As a young man, I tasted the bitter fruits of segregation and racial discrimination, and I didn't like it. I used to ask my parents, my grandparents, and my great grandparents, "Why segregation? Why racial discrimination?" And they would say, "That's the way it is. Don't get in trouble. . . ." But when I heard the words of Dr. King, I knew then that I could strike a blow against segregation and racial discrimination, and I decided to get in trouble. I decided to get in the way. But it was good trouble, necessary trouble. Democracy is not a state. It is an act.

John Lewis, the son of Alabama sharecroppers, was inspired as a teenager by meeting the Reverend Martin Luther King, Jr. Lewis trained in nonviolent methods and organized sit-ins at segregated lunch counters while still a student at Fisk University. He continued to "strike blows against segregation and racial discrimination" for another sixty years.

At the age of twenty-one, Lewis joined the freedom riders, risking his life and being severely beaten by angry mobs. Two years later, he became chairman of the Student Nonviolent Coordinating Committee (SNCC) and organized student activism in the civil rights movement. He was the youngest speaker at the 1963 March on Washington and the most explicit in terms of racial demands. In 1965, as Lewis and Hosea Williams were leading more than six hundred peaceful protesters over the Edmund Pettus Bridge in Selma, Alabama, to demonstrate the need for voting rights, state troopers attacked the marchers, an event that became known as "Bloody Sunday." The violent racism of this event helped hasten the passage of the Voting Rights Act of 1965.

Despite more than forty arrests and serious injuries, John Lewis remained an unrelenting advocate of nonviolence. As the representative in the U.S. House of Representatives for Georgia's Fifth Congressional District from 1987 to 2020, he remained committed to a global vision in which all people can share in the wealth of the Earth. In his autobiography, *Walking with the Wind,* Lewis observed, "Children holding hands, walking with the wind. That is America to me—not just the movement for civil rights but the endless struggle to respond with decency, dignity and a sense of all the challenges that face us as a nation, as a whole. . . . a concept called the Beloved Community."

As a passionately outspoken critic of the Bush administration's military occupation of Iraq, Lewis said, ". . . I must make it plain and clear that as a human being, as a citizen of the world, as a citizen of America, as a Member of Congress, as an individual committed to a world at peace with itself, I will not and I cannot in good conscience vote for another dollar or another dime to support this war."

Lewis received a Backbone Award for his efforts to convince Congress to oppose the Bush administration's actions in the Middle East. He said that the struggle to create the Beloved Community, a just society "at peace with itself," is a struggle of a lifetime.

John Lewis died on July 17, 2020, while still serving in the U.S. Congress, "making good trouble" to his last breath.

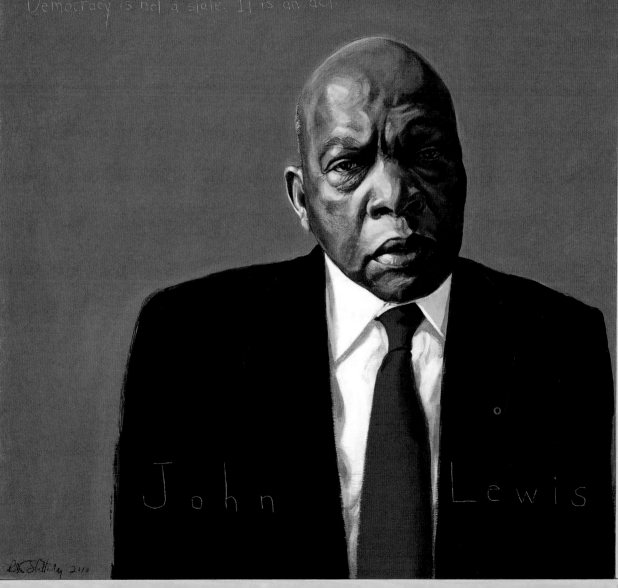

As a young man, I tasted the bitter fruits of segregation and racial discrimination and I didn't like it. I used to ask my parents, my grandparents, and great grandparents, "Why segregation? Why racial discrimination?" And they would say, "That's the way it is. Don't get in trouble." But when I heard the words of Dr. King, I knew then that I could strike a blow against segregation and racial discrimination, and I decided to get in trouble I decided to get in the way. But it was good trouble, necessary trouble.
Democracy is not a state. It is an act.

John   Lewis

Abraham Lincoln

Sixteenth president of the United States; b. 1809, d. 1865

As I would not be a slave, so I would not be a master. This expresses my idea of democracy.

Abraham Lincoln is often described as America's best—and most popular—president. Republicans and Democrats alike claim Honest Abe as their own. Yet Lincoln was a complicated human being and his presidency was the most controversial in American history. After he was elected, seven southern states seceded in protest between 1860 and 1861, effectively launching the Civil War. He was the commander in chief of the Union army during a war that took the lives of at least 620,000 Americans. He suspended the civil liberty of habeas corpus and instituted the first national military draft. He was so controversial that after winning office, he had to sneak into Washington on a secret train to avoid a suspected assassination plot, and when he left, it was in a coffin, the victim of a Confederate sympathizer's bullet.

American politicians like to cast themselves as "of the people," but few have come from beginnings as humble as Lincoln's. He was born on the Kentucky frontier in 1809 in a dirt-floor log cabin with one window, one door hung on leather hinges, and a primitive stick and mud chimney. One of his good friends remembered him as "a long tall raw boned boy—odd and gawky." His clothes rarely fit. One country observer wrote, "Between the shoe and Sock & his britches—made of buckskin there was bare & naked 6 or more inches of Abe Lincoln shin bone." But the ragged appearance veiled an intellectually ravenous mind. He read everything he could get his hands on, and in his mid-twenties, he taught himself law, receiving his license to practice in 1836.

Lincoln was not an unqualified champion of equality. Elected to the Illinois House of Representatives in 1834, he made his mark as a politician who fought against both the extension of slavery and against the full and immediate equality of Blacks advocated by the radical abolitionists. As a congressman from Illinois, he voted to exclude slavery from the territories recently taken from Mexico in the Mexican-American War, and as president, he voted to abolish the slave trade in Washington, D.C. But in 1854, Lincoln declared, "Free them, and make them politically and socially our equals? My own feelings will not admit of this." And in his 1861 inaugural address, he argued that he had no constitutional power to end slavery, nor could he repeal the Fugitive Slave Act.

How should we understand Lincoln's position on race? Was he a wartime leader who signed the 1863 Emancipation Proclamation only to help preserve the Union? Or was he a champion of equality? Can one be against slavery and yet still be a racist?

What we can say is that Lincoln's actions as president managed to preserve the union of states while ending slavery within that union. In light of Lincoln's persistent faith in the Declaration of Independence, perhaps this is his legacy: a determination to honor America's founding ideals, emphasizing the ever-unfinished obligation of every American to struggle toward those self-evident truths that all people are created equal.

As I would not be a slave, so I would not be a master. This expresses my idea of democracy.

Abraham Lincoln

Oren Lyons

Native-American faithkeeper, human rights advocate, environmental activist; b. 1930

The law says if you poison the water, you'll die. The law says that if you poison the air, you'll suffer. The law says if you degrade where you live, you'll suffer. . . . If you don't learn that, you can only suffer. There's no discussion with this law.

Oren Lyons is a member of the Onondaga and Seneca nations of the Iroquois Confederacy. As an activist for Indigenous and environmental justice, Lyons works with communities across the globe. As a faithkeeper, he upholds the history and traditions of the Turtle Clan of the Onondaga and Seneca. He often addresses modern-day conflicts by sharing traditional views on the laws of nature. When he says "You can't negotiate with a beetle," he implies that nature will respond to climate change whether or not humans do.

Oren Lyons was born and raised on Onondaga and Seneca reservations in upstate New York. He later served in the U.S. Army before receiving a scholarship to Syracuse University. At Syracuse, he was an All-American athlete in lacrosse, a sport he continued playing with club teams for many years after graduating. Lyons's athletic career was jump-started during his childhood; lacrosse is traditionally played by the Iroquois.

After graduating from college with a degree in fine arts, Lyons moved to New York City to launch his career in commercial art.

In the 1960s, Lyons joined what has been dubbed the "Red Power movement," a group of Native American activists who came together across tribal lines to draw attention to Indigenous rights and struggles. Upon reaching his forties, he returned to the land of his birth in upstate New York and to the cultural heritage of the Onondaga.

Throughout the 1970s, Lyons took a leadership role in Native American rights events, including the Trail of Broken Treaties, a caravan that traveled to Washington, D.C., to confront the Bureau of Indian Affairs. Increasingly focused on traditional practices and native culture, Lyons helped convene the Traditional Circle of Indian Elders and Youth, which still meets annually.

Lyons's activist work connected him with other Indigenous groups around the globe, including the Maori in New Zealand. He helped establish the United Nations working group on Indigenous peoples in 1982. In remarks to the UN General Assembly in 1992, Lyons highlighted the Indigenous peoples' struggle in an era of unrestrained growth, addressing key areas for improvement.

In addition to his international work, Lyons served as professor of American Studies and director of the Native American Studies Program at the State University of New York at Buffalo. As a scholar, he has published many books and articles, including children's books. He edited *Exiled in the Land of the Free* (1992), which made the case for the influence of the Iroquois Confederacy's values on American democracy and the Constitution.

Now retired from teaching, Lyons continues to inspire generations through his leadership in the Traditional Circle of Indian Elders and Youth and public speaking.

Lyons's dedication to the cause of Indigenous and environmental rights has garnered him many accolades, including an honorary degree from his alma mater, Syracuse University. Institutions, including the Rosa Parks Institute for Human Rights and the National Audubon Society, have also recognized Lyons's work. He received the Ellis Island Medal of Honor in 1990.

Oren Lyons

The law says if you   poison the water, you'll die.
The law says that if   you poison the air, you'll suffer.
The law says if you degrade   where you live, you'll suffer...
If you don't learn that, then you can only suffer.
There's no discussion with this law.

Janice Mirikitani

Community activist, poet, editor; b. 1941

I found that my wounds begin to heal when the voices of those endangered by silence are given power. The silence of hopelessness, of despair buried in the depths of poverty, violence, racism . . . are more deadly than bullets. . . . The gift of light, in our compassion, our listening, our works of love . . . is the gift of life to ourselves.

Janice Mirikitani is the founding president of the Glide Foundation, where she and her husband, the Reverend Cecil Williams, have achieved worldwide recognition for their groundbreaking efforts to empower San Francisco's poor and marginalized communities. Their work inspires people to make meaningful changes in their lives, breaking the cycle of poverty. During Glide's first forty years, Mirikitani and Williams built eighty-seven comprehensive programs—providing education, recovery support, primary and mental health care, job training, housing, and human services. Mirikitani's passion has been to create programs for women and families as they struggle with issues of substance abuse, rape, incest, domestic violence, the AIDS crisis, single parenting, and child care. The couple's book, *Beyond the Possible* (2013), tells Glide's story, reflecting on fifty years of creating radical social change.

Mirikitani and her family were interned in the Rohwer War Relocation Center, in Arkansas, during World War II. As Japanese immigrant farmers, they were swept up in the wartime mass internment of Japanese Americans. Undeterred, Mirikitani went on to graduate from UCLA, earned a teaching credential from UC Berkeley, and has received two honorary doctorates.

Mirikitani is also San Francisco's second poet laureate, appointed in 2000. She has written four books of poetry: *Awake in the River; Shedding Silence; We, the Dangerous;* and *Love Works.* And she has edited nine landmark anthologies, providing platforms for writers of color, women, youth, and children.

Mirikitani began serving as a commissioner on the San Francisco Arts Commission in 1996 and was reappointed by Mayor Newsom in 2004. She is the recipient of over forty awards and honors, including the Governor and First Lady's Conference on Women and Families' Minerva Award, San Francisco State University's Distinguished Alumnae Award, the San Francisco Chamber of Commerce's Lifetime Achievement Ebbie Award, the prestigious American Book Lifetime Achievement Award for Literature, and the University of California at San Francisco Chancellor's Medal of Honor Award.

I found that my wounds begin to heal when the voices of those endangered by silence are given power. The silence of hopelessness, of despair buried in the depths of poverty, violence, racism... are more deadly than bullets...
The gift of light, in our compassion, our listening, our works of love...
is the gift of life to ourselves

Janice Mirikitani

Sherri Mitchell, Weh'na Ha'mu Kwasset

Lawyer, Indigenous and human rights activist; b. 1969

Rights and responsibilities cannot be separated. Every right that we stand upon must be balanced by a set of corresponding responsibilities. We cannot legitimately make a demand unless we are willing to take responsibility for creating a world where that demand can be met.

Sherri Mitchell is the daughter of two First Nations, the Penobscot and the Passamaquoddy tribes, whose sovereign territories are found within the borders of the state of Maine. Both nations are members of the Wabanaki Confederacy.

Raised on the Penobscot Indian Island Reservation, Mitchell inherited tradition, culture, and a deep sense of responsibility to her people. Her Passamaquoddy grandmothers spoke their Indigenous language fluently. Sherri spent time with them preparing materials for basket making, harvesting and preparing traditional foods, learning about kindness and charity, and hearing the stories of her people's history and connection to place. Her grandfathers were tribal leaders and two of her great-grandfathers held the office of chief of the Penobscot Nation. Her maternal grandfather, Ted Mitchell, with whom she was especially close, founded the Native American Studies Program and the Wabanaki Center, a "gathering place for indigenous scholars," at the University of Maine.

From her elders, Mitchell gained an understanding that the Earth doesn't need us but that we need the Earth. As an Indigenous rights lawyer, Mitchell does not presume that we are the stewards of the Earth; rather, our job is to be stewards of a way of life that fosters harmony and balance among all living things.

Mitchell teaches that everyone has been hurt by our shared history; the oppressed, the oppressors, and even the witnesses have suffered. The Western European model of the "supremacy of the individual," says Mitchell, "is completely separate from the Indigenous way of life and a sure path to suicide for the entire species. We have to rebuild community, share resources, grow food, protect water sources and create our own energy." In other words, we will survive and prosper together or not at all.

Sherri Mitchell graduated magna cum laude with a bachelor's degree from the University of Maine and received her J.D. and a certificate in Indigenous Peoples Law and Policy from the University of Arizona's James E. Rogers College of Law. She has participated in both the American Indian Ambassador Program and the Udall Native American Congressional Internship Program. In 2010, she received the Mahoney Dunn International Human Rights and Humanitarian Award for research into human rights violations against Indigenous peoples, and she is the 2015 recipient of the Spirit of Maine Award for commitment and excellence in the field of international human rights.

Mitchell is the founding director of the Land Peace Foundation, an organization dedicated to the global protection of Indigenous rights and the preservation of the Indigenous way of life. She speaks and teaches on issues of Indigenous rights, environmental justice, peace building, strategic nonviolence, and spiritual activism throughout the United States and Canada. She is the author of *Sacred Instructions: Indigenous Wisdom for Living Spirit-Based Change* (2018).

Sherri Mitchell

Rights and responsibilities cannot be separated. Every right that we stand upon must be balanced by a set of corresponding responsibilities. We cannot legitimately make a demand unless we are willing to take responsibility for creating a world where that demand can be met.

Robert Shetterly 2016

Bob Moses

Organizer, educator; b. 1935

Well, I don't think that the Democratic Party to this day has confronted the issue of bringing into its ranks the kind of people that were represented by the Mississippi Freedom Democratic Party. That is the real underclass of this country. The Democratic Party primarily has organized around the middle class. And we were challenging them not only on racial grounds but we were challenging them on the existence of a whole group of people who are the underclass of this country, white and black, who are not represented. And they weren't prepared to hear that; I don't know if they heard.

Historian Taylor Branch described Bob Moses in this way: "I think his influence is almost on par with Martin Luther King, and yet he's almost totally unknown." Through his many years as a civil rights organizer, Moses was self-effacing, observant, and sensitive. These characteristics kept him out of the spotlight but made him a highly effective leader.

Born on January 23, 1935, in New York City's Harlem, Moses was the son of a janitor. He grew up in a Harlem housing project but received a high-quality public education. Academic achievement got him admitted to Stuyvesant High School, one of New York City's best public schools. He earned a scholarship to Hamilton College and a master's degree and Ph.D. in philosophy from Harvard. He spent the early years of his career teaching math at Horace Mann School, an exclusive prep school in New York, and later taught math in Tanzania.

Despite his quiet demeanor, Moses became an important figure in the civil rights movement, working with Dr. King and the Southern Christian Leadership Conference (SCLC). As the head of the Student Nonviolent Coordinating Committee (SNCC) Mississippi Project in the early 1960s, Moses organized voter registration drives, sit-ins, and Freedom Schools, which led to significant gains in voting rights for Black Mississippians. He was heavily influenced by Ella Baker, who believed that civil rights movements should belong to the people, not to the leaders. Organizers should stay in the background, developing trust and guiding from behind as people define their priorities and reach toward their goals.

In 1964, Moses, along with Fannie Lou Hamer, founded the Mississippi Freedom Democratic Party (MFDP), which challenged the all-white Mississippi delegation to the 1964 presidential convention. Although the MFDP didn't win any seats, they forced the integration of the mainstream Democratic Party and brought representation to previously disenfranchised people.

Moses was awarded the MacArthur "Genius Grant" in 1982, then moved forward with a new civil rights agenda: education. He started the Algebra Project, helping the lowest-performing students to prepare for college math and twenty-first-century careers. The Algebra Project began at one school in Cambridge, Massachusetts, and, by the late 1990s, it had expanded to more than two hundred middle schools nationwide.

In his book *Radical Equations: Civil Rights from Mississippi to the Algebra Project* (2001), Moses explains: ". . . everyone said sharecroppers were apathetic until we got them demanding to vote. That finally got attention. Here, where kids are falling wholesale through the cracks—or chasms— . . . people say they don't want to learn. The only ones who can dispel that notion are the kids themselves. They . . . have to demand what everyone says they don't want."

Moses has called for a constitutional amendment establishing quality public school education as a civil right.

Bob   Moses

Well, I don't think that the Democratic Party to this day has
confronted the issue of bringing into its ranks the kind of people
that were represented by the Mississippi Freedom Democratic
Party. That is the real underclass of this country. The Democratic
Party primarily has organized around the middle class. And we
were challenging them not only on racial grounds but we
were challenging them on the existence of a whole group of people
who are the underclass of this country, white and black, who are
not represented.

                      And they weren't prepared to hear that; I don't
know if they heard.

Carlos Muñoz, Jr.

Scholar, educator; b. 1939

As Latinos, we are not islands unto ourselves. Our past and present struggles for social and economic justice have been directly connected with those of all oppressed peoples. We know we are an indigenous people. But we must also know that we are African, Asian, Middle Eastern, and European. We are of all faiths. We are America!

Carlos Muñoz, Jr., the son of poor Mexican immigrants, was born in the "segundo barrio" of El Paso, Texas, and raised in the barrios of East Los Angeles, California. He overcame poverty to earn a Ph.D. and become a prominent scholar and pioneer in establishing Chicano Studies programs in higher education. He is professor emeritus in the Department of Ethnic Studies at the University of California, Berkeley. His best-known work, *Youth, Identity, Power: The Chicano Movement* (1989, revised 2007), has become the classic study of the movement.

As a prominent leader of the Chicano civil rights movement, Muñoz was one of thirteen activists indicted in 1968 for conspiracy. The group had been targeted for organizing nonviolent student protests against racial/ethnic educational inequality in the schools of East Los Angeles. Each faced sixty-six years in prison. It took two years for the high courts of California to decide they were protected from prosecution by the free speech clause of the First Amendment to the U.S. Constitution.

Since then, Muñoz has served as a leading organizer for various multiracial coalitions, including the Faculty for Human Rights in Central America, the Faculty Against Apartheid in South Africa, and the Rainbow Coalition. He cofounded the Institute for Multiracial Justice in San Francisco and Latinos Unidos, a grassroots community organization in Berkeley, California. He also cofounded the Families for Multicultural Education in Albany, California.

Muñoz maintains that his family has always been his "most cherished blessing." As the father of five children and grandfather of eight, he has been an outspoken critic of what he calls the "government's terrorist war" against Latino immigrant families. ". . . Immigration Customs Enforcement (ICE) regularly conducts nationwide raids in workplaces and homes of immigrant workers to arrest those they suspect are undocumented immigrants. Those with legal status are also often harassed, arrested, and sometimes deported without trial. The raids have resulted in the tragic breakup of many families, leaving their U.S.-born children homeless when parents are deported without the knowledge of their children."

As a Vietnam War veteran, and a member of Veterans for Peace, Muñoz has been an outspoken critic of all wars and U.S. intervention throughout the world. "Our government should be a Democracy that declares war on poverty at home and abroad and not on sovereign nations that do not threaten our nation's freedom."

Muñoz advocates a new politics for the twenty-first century that is "inclusive of gender, race, ethnicity, class, sexuality, and disability . . . framed with a vision of an authentic multiracial and multiethnic democracy that will promote social justice, human rights, and peace at home and abroad." He believes it will take an arduous struggle to realize his vision, but he says, ". . . victory is in the struggle."

Carlos Muñoz, Jr.

As Latinos, we are not islands unto ourselves. Our past and present struggles for social and economic justice have been directly connected with those of all oppressed peoples. We know we are an indigenous people. But we must also know that we are African, Asian, Middle Eastern, and European. We are of all faiths. We are America!

Pauli Murray

Attorney, minister, author; b. 1910, d. 1985

And since, as a human being, I cannot allow myself to be fragmented into a Negro at one time, a woman at another, or worker at another, I must find a unifying principle in all these movements to which I can adhere. . . . This, it seems to me, is not only good politics but may be the price of survival.

Anna Pauline "Pauli" Murray was born in Baltimore, Maryland, on November 20, 1910. Losing both parents during her adolescence, Murray was raised by grandparents and an aunt in Durham, North Carolina. After high school, Murray moved to New York City. As a female, she could not attend Columbia University, her first choice. Unable to afford Columbia's sister school, Barnard College, Murray enrolled at Hunter College ("the poor girl's Radcliffe"), where she earned a bachelor's degree in English in 1933.

During the Great Depression, Murray worked with both the Women's Auxiliary of the Civilian Conservation Corps (CCC) and the Works Progress Administration (WPA). In 1940, Murray and another Fellowship of Reconciliation (FOR) member, Adelene McBean, were arrested (fifteen years before Rosa Parks) for refusing to give up their seats on a segregated bus in Petersburg, Virginia.

Rejected by the University of North Carolina School of Law on the basis of race, Murray enrolled at Howard University's law school in 1941, the only woman in her class. At Howard, Murray coined the term "Jane Crow" to describe the discrimination she faced as a woman. She finished first in her class. Rejected by Harvard for post-graduate studies because of her gender, Murray got an LL.M. degree at the University of California, Berkeley, then worked as a California deputy attorney general, another first for an African American, regardless of gender.

Commended by Thurgood Marshall as a critical guide to attorneys working on civil rights cases, Murray's 1951 book, *States' Laws on Race and Color,* laid out a definitive framework for challenging state segregation laws. Murray wrote more books, then taught law at universities in Ghana and the United States and American Studies at Brandeis University. She earned a J.S.D. (doctor of juridical science) at Yale University in 1965, the first African American to achieve that degree at Yale.

At the height of the civil rights movement, Murray offered a critique of the 1963 March on Washington (organized primarily by her colleague Bayard Rustin): "It is indefensible to call a national march on Washington and send out a call which contains the name of not a single woman leader." John F. Kennedy appointed Murray to the Presidential Commission on the Status of Women, and, in 1966, she became a cofounder of the National Organization for Women (NOW).

After her years at Brandeis, Murray switched paths and embarked on a new career in the Episcopal Church. She was ordained at the National Cathedral in Washington, D.C., as an Episcopal priest, another first for an African American woman. Murray served primarily in Baltimore, but also in Washington, D.C., and Pittsburgh, where she died from pancreatic cancer on July 1, 1985.

Open about her romantic relationships with women and unapologetic about her non-gender-conforming appearance, Murray was marginalized by civil rights movement historians. As the nation's acceptance of the LGBTQ community grows, we are learning more about the full and rich lives of those who, like Murray, made overlooked but formidable contributions to American history.

And since as a human being I cannot allow myself to be fragmented into a Negro at one time, a woman at another or worker at another. I must find a unifying principle in all these movements to which I can adhere ... This it seems to me, is not only good politics but also may be the price of survival.

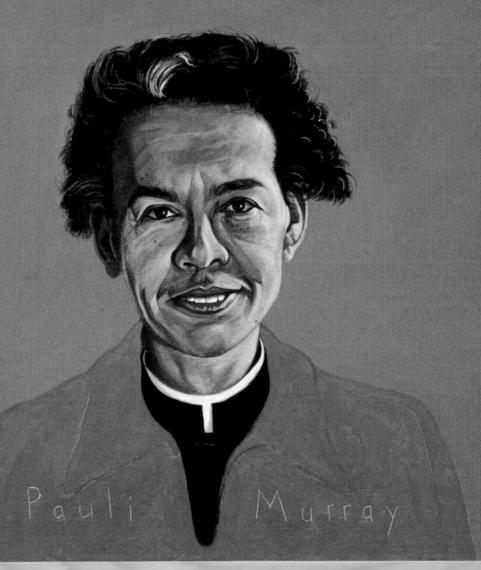

Pauli   Murray

Bree Newsome

Activist, singer, filmmaker; b. 1985

*I removed the flag not only in defiance of those who enslaved my ancestors in the southern
United States, but also in defiance of the oppression that continues against black people globally. . . .
I did it for all the fierce black women on the front lines of the movement and for all
the little black girls who are watching us. I did it because I am free.*

On June 27, 2015, Americans watched an unnamed woman scale a thirty-foot pole and remove the Confederate flag from the State House in Columbia, South Carolina. This was Brittany "Bree" Newsome.

Newsome is a graduate of New York University's Tisch School of the Arts and holds a BFA degree in film and television. While in high school, Newsome composed music for the Baltimore Choral Arts Society. In college, she won several film competitions and since has released an EP titled *#StayStrong: A Love Song to Freedom Fighters.* For Newsome, art is activism.

The courageous thirty-year-old filmmaker, activist, and songstress's action took place one day after President Obama eulogized the Honorable Reverend Clementa Pinckney, a member of the South Carolina Senate and one of nine shooting victims at Mother Emmanuel AME Church in Charleston, South Carolina. Newsome worked with a team of ten people who strategically planned to film the removal of the flag so that the world could see "good trouble" in action. Newsome credits Todd Zimmer, a fellow organizer, for envisioning the video, which had such a powerful impact. As she scaled the flagpole, Newsome shouted, "You come against me with hatred . . . I come against you in the name of God. This flag comes down today!" On her way down, carrying the Confederate flag, she recited the Lord's Prayer and Psalm 27.

Asked by a reporter why she removed the flag, Newsome said, "We removed the flag today because we can't wait any longer. We can't continue like this another day. It's time for a new chapter where we are sincere about dismantling white supremacy and building toward true racial justice and equality. Every day that the flag is up there is an endorsement of hate."

As she descended with the flag, Newsome and another activist, James Ian Tyson, were arrested. Hours later, the flag was raised again. Rallies by white supremacists and advocates of the flag were held in cities around the country. In less than twenty-four hours, the hashtag #FreeBree surfaced on the Internet with coverage of the historic moment; 4,943 people raised $125,705 on Indiegogo to support whatever financial obligations Newsome might face in court. The flag was permanently removed by the state legislature on July 10, 2015.

A year later, Newsome explained why the video was key. "It mattered that scaling the flagpole was difficult. The physical battle to climb up there and get that flag was like the struggle to dismantle systemic racism. Nothing about it is easy." She continues to take her message directly to the people through a wide range of speaking engagements and social media and blog posts. Her message is that you, too, can find your "flagpole moment."

Bree Newsome

I removed the flag not only in defiance of those who enslaved my ancestors in the southern United States, but also in defiance of the oppression that continues against black people globally. I did it for all the fierce black women on the front lines of the movement and for all the little black girls who are watching us.

I did it because I am free.

Rosa Parks

Seamstress, civil rights leader; b. 1913, d. 2005

The only tired I was, was tired of giving in.

osa Parks, the matriarch of the civil rights movement, has been described as an old woman too tired to move when ordered to give up her seat to a white person on a city bus in Montgomery, Alabama, in December 1955. However, Parks later said, "I was not old, although some people have an image of me as being old then. I was forty-two." And "the only tired I was, was tired of giving in." Parks's sentiment represented the view of the millions of African Americans, and their allies, who set out to end legal segregation in the mid-1900s.

Parks was born Rosa Louise McCauley in Tuskegee, Alabama, on February 4, 1913. Following her parents' separation, Parks moved with her mother and younger brother to her maternal grandparents' home in Pine Level, Alabama, just outside of Montgomery. She was educated at Montgomery's Industrial School for Girls. At age sixteen, Parks suspended her studies to help support her family.

Parks became an activist for racial equality gradually. In 1932, she married Raymond Parks, a Montgomery barber who was active in the local NAACP chapter. With her husband's encouragement, Parks completed her high school education the following year. Parks joined the NAACP in 1943, and began serving as secretary to Montgomery chapter president E. D. Nixon. In the summer of 1955, she attended a training session for activists at the Highlander Folk School (now the Highlander Center) in Monteagle, Tennessee.

On December 1 of that year, following her day of work at Montgomery Fair department store, Parks boarded a city bus and sat in the "colored" section. As the number of white passengers grew, the bus driver moved the aisle sign marking the "colored" section, increasing the number of seats available to white passengers. Parks decided that she was not going to get up and move to a row behind her. The bus driver called the police, and Parks was arrested for violating Montgomery's segregation laws.

On December 5, the day of Parks's trial, a one-day boycott of the Montgomery city buses was called. Parks was found guilty of disorderly conduct and violating the segregation law. And the boycott was extended, leading to the creation of the Montgomery Improvement Association (MIA), led by a young Martin Luther King, Jr. The African American community of Montgomery boycotted the buses for over a year, until December 20, 1956, after their case, *Browder v. Gayle,* was decided by the U.S. Supreme Court, ruling that segregated seating on public buses was unconstitutional.

Parks was awarded the Presidential Medal of Freedom in 1996, as well as the Congressional Gold Medal in 1999, for her role in the civil rights movement.

Rosa Parks died on October 24, 2005. On October 30, President George W. Bush ordered all U.S. flags to be flown at half-staff in her honor. Parks was the first woman and the second African American to lie in state in the rotunda of the U.S. Capitol. On February 27, 2013, a statue of Parks was unveiled in the National Statuary Hall in the U.S. Capitol.

Rosa Parks

The only tired I was,
was tired of giving in.

Eva Paterson

Civil rights lawyer; b. 1949

Race is the great taboo in our society. We are afraid to talk about it. White folks fear their un-spoken views will be deemed racist. People of color are filled with sorrow and rage at unrighted wrongs. Drowning in silence, we are brothers and sisters drowning each other. Once we decide to transform ourselves from fearful caterpillars into courageous butterflies, we will be able to bridge the racial gulf and move forward together towards a bright and colorful future.

Twenty-one-year-old Eva Paterson captured the nation's attention when she debated Vice President Spiro T. Agnew on television in 1970. As student body president of Illinois's Northwestern University, she respectfully disagreed with the second most powerful man in America and, by most measures, won the debate.

Accused by Agnew of promoting violent protests of the Vietnam War and racial discrimination, Paterson objected, asserting her commitment to nonviolence. Then she charged Agnew with making things worse by scaring people: "You're making people afraid of their own children. . . . They're your children, they're my parents' children, they're the children of this country. Yet you're making people afraid of them. This is the greatest disservice. . . . When you make people afraid of each other, you isolate people. Maybe this is your goal, but I think this could only have a disastrous effect on the country."

It wasn't the last time Patterson would speak truth to power and win the day.

A few years later, armed with a law degree from UC Berkeley's Boalt Hall School of Law, she began her fight for social and economic justice. She sued the Oakland (California) police because they did so little to help battered women. She won that case and saw it become the model for how police departments across America deal with spousal abuse.

For Paterson, combating domestic violence was personal. "I come from a home with a lot of violence,"
explains Paterson. ". . . when I was very young, I really tried to protect my mother from my father. . . . so I think some sense of being a warrior was being instilled at that point. . . ."

Other lawsuits led to desegregating the San Francisco school system, putting Blacks and women on the force of the San Francisco Fire Department, and eliminating discrimination that kept Asian Americans from gaining white-collar jobs with the federal government.

"It's important to embody Dr. King's notion that an injury to one is an injury to all," says Paterson. When she's asked why she works so hard for the benefit of others, she replies, "I don't think I have a choice. . . . and I know I have the ability to make a difference or to connect with people who can make a difference."

Paterson now heads her own organization, the Equal Justice Society, with a sharp focus on building coalitions. "In my view, coalitions are not optional, they're essential. . . . We all share a common vision of the world we're trying to create, so we need to get out of our silos."

Paterson's lifelong activism includes cofounding a shelter for battered women in Oakland and serving as a member of the Lawyers' Committee for Civil Rights, as vice president of the ACLU National Board, and as chair of both Equal Rights Advocates and the San Francisco Bar Association.

Race is the great taboo in our society. We are afraid to talk about it.
White folks fear their unspoken views will be deemed racist. People of color
are filled with sorrow and rage at unrighted wrongs. Drowning in silence,
we are brothers and sisters drowning each other. Once we decide to
transform ourselves from fearful caterpillars into courageous butterflies,
we will be able to bridge the racial gulf and move forward together
towards a bright and colorful future.

Eva Paterson

Ai-jen Poo

Organizer of domestic workers; b. 1974

The twenty-first century way to create social change is to determine where we can create win-win-win situations around our values. These values are simple: ensuring we can take care of ourselves, our families, our communities, and future generations to come.

In 2012, Ai-jen Poo was named one of *Time* magazine's most influential people and made *Newsweek*'s list of "150 Fearless Women." Founder and president of the National Domestic Workers Alliance (NDWA), Poo's prominence is in the success of her fight for the rights of domestic workers.

It's Poo's respect for all sides in labor disputes that has caught people's attention. "I believe that love is the most powerful force for change in the world. I often compare great campaigns to great love affairs because they're an incredible container for transformation. You can change policy, but you also change relationships and people in the process."

Strengthening the connection between domestic workers and their employers has led to major social change in the form of legislation, policy, and improved working conditions. "Theirs is the work that makes all other work possible, because without it many professionals could not go to their jobs."

Poo's family taught her the value of social justice. Her parents, a scientist and a doctor, immigrated to the United States from Taiwan, where her father was a pro-democracy activist. After growing up in California and Connecticut, Ai-jen Poo's career as an activist began when she was majoring in women's studies at Columbia University. She joined one hundred fellow students in an occupation of the university library, demanding that Columbia develop a curriculum reflecting the rich diversity of the student body.

As a result, Columbia established a Center for the Study of Ethnicity and Race. "Working with a really diverse group of students around our shared goals gave me a sense of how powerful campaigns can be if they're strategic."

After college, Poo took a job at the Committee Against Anti-Asian Violence, where she learned about the vulnerability of domestic workers. These women inspired her. Poo cofounded New York City's Domestic Workers United (DWU) in 2000. By 2007, the DWU had grown into the National Domestic Workers Alliance. Poo's first big breakthrough with the NDWA happened in 2010, when the New York state legislature passed the Domestic Workers Bill of Rights, which legitimated domestic workers and gave them new rights, including vacation time and overtime pay. Three years later, the U.S. Department of Labor extended the Fair Labor Standards Act's minimum wage and overtime protections to most of the nation's workers who provide essential home care.

In 2014, Poo was awarded a MacArthur fellowship, "a five-year grant . . . to fund her vibrant, worker-led movement." In June 2019, a National Domestic Workers Bill of Rights was introduced in the U.S. Congress. As of late 2020, NDWA membership had expanded to over sixty affiliate organizations and local chapters and thousands of individual members, while nine states and two cities had passed laws protecting domestic workers.

The Twenty-first century way to create social change is to determine where we can create win-win-win situations around our values. These values are simple: ensuring we can take care of ourselves, our families, our communities, and future generations to come.

Ai-jen Poo

Robert Shetterly 2013

Bernice Johnson Reagon

Singer, composer, scholar, social activist; b. 1942

The changing of my voice came after jail. . . . It was bigger than I'd ever heard it before. It had this ringing in it. It filled all the space of the church. I thought that was because I had been to jail. It was because I had stepped outside of the safety zone. . . . I tell people, if you don't sometimes walk through trouble, you'll never get to meet the rest of yourself. . . . And maybe if I'd never gone to jail, I would not have ever gotten to know that part of my singing. It was a blessing.

In 1961, Bernice Johnson Reagon was expelled from Albany State College in southwest Georgia after being jailed for her participation in a civil rights protest. But, school officials could not keep her down; this young woman rose to become a world-famous singer, composer, scholar, and social activist.

Born on October 4, 1942, Bernice Johnson Reagon grew up in a tight-knit African American community outside of Albany, Georgia. Discrimination ran rampant. As the child of a minister, Reagon grew up with the Black choral tradition, developing a strong sense of the beauty and healing power of music.

After a brief time at Spelman College, Reagon joined the Freedom Singers, touring to raise money for the Student Nonviolent Coordinating Committee (SNCC). As a member of SNCC and the National Association for the Advancement of Colored People (NAACP), she participated in voter registration drives and antisegregation protests.

In 1963, she met and married fellow Freedom Singer Cordell Reagon. They had a son and a daughter together. After divorcing in 1967, Reagon decided to complete her college education. She returned to Spelman and graduated in 1970. She was awarded a Ford Fellowship and moved to Washington, D.C., to earn her Ph.D. in history at Howard University. During this time, she grew as a scholar and an artist, working as vocal director of the D.C. Black Repertory Theater.

In 1973, Reagon founded Sweet Honey in the Rock, an a cappella singing group of African American women. While still performing with the group, she became director of the Smithsonian's program in Black American Culture, and later, she was appointed curator at the National Museum of American History. As a scholar, Reagon has produced books, articles, documentaries, and presentations that preserve and celebrate African American music and culture.

Reagon has been awarded fourteen honorary doctorates and several awards in the arts and humanities. In 1989, she was awarded the MacArthur "Genius Grant" for "extraordinary originality and dedication in creative pursuits."

Retiring from Sweet Honey in the Rock in 2004, Reagon continued to perform. She describes herself as a "songtalker, one who balances talk and song in the creation of a live performance conversation with those who gather within the sound of my voice."

In an interview with Bill Moyers, she explained the value of African American culture: "When the culture is strong, you've got this consistency where black people can grow up in these places with this voice just resonating about our special-ness in the universe."

Over a lifetime of work as a preservationist, artist, and performer, Bernice Johnson Reagon has served to inspire and empower people all over the world.

The changing of my voice came after jail... It was bigger than I'd ever heard it before. It had this ringing in it. It filled all the space of the church. I thought that was because I had been to jail. It was because I had stepped outside of the safety zone... I tell people, if you don't sometimes walk through trouble, you'll never get to meet the rest of yourself... And maybe if I'd never gone to jail, I would not have ever gotten to know that part of my singing. It was a blessing.

Bernice
Johnson
Reagon

Rob Shetterly 2013

Paul Robeson

Singer, writer, civil rights activist; b. 1898, d. 1976

The talents of an artist, small or great, are God given. They've nothing to do with him as a private person; they're nothing to be proud of. They're just a sacred trust. . . . Having been given, I must give. Man shall not live by bread alone, and what the farmer does I must do. I must feed the people—with my songs.

Born in Princeton, New Jersey, Paul Robeson was the son of a minister who had been a runaway slave. A keen student and gifted athlete, Robeson won a scholarship to Rutgers, was elected to Phi Beta Kappa in his junior year, and graduated in 1919 as class valedictorian. He was also an All-American football player who put himself through Columbia Law School by playing professional football on weekends.

When a stenographer at his New York law firm refused to take dictation from a "nigger," he abandoned his legal career in favor of the stage. He joined the Provincetown Players, where he won praise for his performance in the title role of Eugene O'Neill's *Emperor Jones.* Success followed success. His generation knew him best for his portrayal of Othello onstage and for his bass rendition of "Ol' Man River" in stage and screen versions of *Show Boat.*

Traveling and performing abroad offered Robeson new perspectives. In his 1958 autobiography, *Here I Stand,* he wrote that "the essential character of a nation is determined . . . by the common people, and that the common people of all nations are truly brothers in the great family of mankind." This perception inspired him to look beyond the traditional American work songs and spirituals; he began to learn more languages so that he could sing folk songs from other cultures. In the Soviet Union of the 1930s, he found a country free of racial prejudice: "Here, for the first time in my life I walk in full human dignity." When he returned to the United States, Robeson became an outspoken critic of racism. He refused to sing before segregated audiences and led an antilynching campaign.

Many artists and writers who were drawn to communism in the 1930s had renounced it by the end of the decade, when Stalin signed a pact with Hitler. Paul Robeson did not, and his acceptance of the 1952 Stalin Peace Prize made him an outcast in an America gripped by the Cold War. When a congressional committee asked him why he hadn't stayed in the Soviet Union, he replied, "Because my father was a slave, and my people died to build this country, and I am going to stay right here, and have a part of it just like you." His passport was revoked from 1950 to 1958. He was blacklisted as a performer and unable to earn a good living.

Paul Robeson once said, "The artist must elect to fight for Freedom or for Slavery. I have made my choice. I had no alternative."

Paul Robeson

The talents of an artist, small or great, are God given.
They've nothing to do with him as a private person; They're
nothing to be proud of. They're just a sacred trust...
Having been given, I must give. Man shall not live by
bread alone, and what the farmer does I must do. I
must feed the people — with my songs.

Bayard Rustin

Organizer, activist; b. 1912, d. 1987

First, what is the dynamic idea of our time? It is the quest for human dignity expressed in many ways—self-determination, freedom from bigotry, and equality of opportunity. If we want human dignity above all else, we cannot get it while we are on our knees, we cannot get it if we are running away, we cannot get it if we are indifferent and unconcerned.

Born on March 17, 1912, in West Chester, Pennsylvania, Bayard Taylor Rustin was raised by his maternal grandparents. His grandmother Julia Rustin, an active member of the NAACP and a Quaker, imparted the values to her grandson that would guide him for the rest of his life. He attended an integrated high school, where he was a star athlete, amazed people with his beautiful singing voice, and ranked at the top of his class.

Rustin moved to Harlem in the 1930s to live with a sister and attend City College. There he was able to express his homosexuality more fully for the first time. He also became active in the Fellowship of Reconciliation (FOR) and began a lifelong mentorship with A. Philip Randolph.

During 1941, Rustin organized Randolph's proposed march on Washington to challenge the lack of employment opportunities for African Americans in the defense industry. Then World War II put Rustin on a collision course with the draft. As a conscientious objector, he spent twenty-eight months behind bars, where he led protests to advance integration and improve prison conditions.

Once released from prison, Rustin joined the Journey of Reconciliation, an integrated team of sixteen men organized to test the 1946 busing integration decision, *Morgan v. Virginia*, which southern states had ignored. Rustin was arrested and sentenced to work on a chain gang in North Carolina, which he did for twenty-two days.

Nine years later, in 1956, Randolph sent Rustin to investigate the Montgomery bus boycott. He worked closely with Dr. King to establish the movement's core value of nonviolence and to create the Southern Christian Leadership Conference (SCLC). Enemies tried to discredit King by exposing Rustin's sexual orientation. Despite this, at Randolph's insistence, Rustin was recruited to organize the 1963 March on Washington. Rustin rallied approximately 250,000 people and provided King the national platform for his famed "I Have a Dream" speech.

Following the passage of the Civil Rights Act of 1964, Rustin wrote "From Protest to Politics," arguing for deeper alignments with the Democratic Party and the labor movement and calling for a racially integrated movement for economic justice. While acting as executive director of the A. Philip Randolph Institute, Rustin lost friends and gained political enemies by prioritizing his support of President Johnson's civil rights initiatives, while others, including Dr. King, took up the cause against the Vietnam War.

Later in life, Rustin advocated for New York City's gay rights bill, which was approved by the city council in 1986.

Rustin died of a heart attack on August 24, 1987, and was survived by his partner, Walter Naegle. Multiple biographies and documentaries have ensured that Rustin's legacy will not be lost. In 2006, the newest high school in West Chester was named for Rustin, and in 2013, he was posthumously awarded the Presidential Medal of Freedom.

First, what is the dynamic idea of our time? It is the quest for human dignity expressed in many ways — self-determination, freedom from bigotry, and equality of opportunity. If we want human dignity above all else, we cannot get it while we are on our knees, we cannot get it if we are running away, we cannot get it if we are indifferent and unconcerned.

Bayard Rustin

Robert Shetterly 2016

Bryan Stevenson

Death row lawyer, writer; b. 1959

The great evil of American slavery was not involuntary servitude but rather the narrative of racial differences we created to legitimize slavery. Because we never dealt with that evil, I don't think slavery ended in 1865, it just evolved.

Bryan Stevenson has said, "Whenever society begins to create policies and laws rooted in fear and anger, there will be abuse and injustice." It is rare for those who are poor and those who are minimized or incarcerated to find a champion who will affirm their humanity. Bryan Stevenson is that rare champion. His weapons are the U.S. Constitution and the accurate recollection of American history.

Stevenson was born on November 14, 1959, to Howard Stevenson, Sr., and Alice (Golden) Stevenson in Milton, Delaware. After spending his earliest school years in a racially segregated school, Stevenson attended the newly integrated Cape Henlopen High School and then entered Eastern University, in St. David's, Pennsylvania, where he studied political science and philosophy.

In the fall of 1981, Stevenson enrolled in a dual-degree program in law and public policy at Harvard Law School and the John F. Kennedy School of Government. There he discovered his professional calling. As a second-year intern with the Atlanta-based Southern Center for Human Rights, Stevenson witnessed the magnitude of problems faced by criminal defendants and inmates. Stevenson has quipped that "capital punishment means 'them without capital get the punishment.'" Upon graduation from Harvard in 1985, Stevenson joined the Southern Center as a staff attorney and was assigned to work in Alabama.

After the congressional funding supporting the Southern Center was eliminated, Stevenson continued the work by establishing the Equal Justice Initiative (EJI) in 1994. The following year, he was awarded a MacArthur fellowship, which he used to support EJI's work of transforming the landscape of the criminal justice system. Stevenson has been particularly effective at combating the draconian criminal penalties imposed on children convicted of crimes. In a series of U.S. Supreme Court cases from 2005 to 2016, the EJI helped to establish that children are constitutionally protected from receiving death sentences and mandatory life sentences without parole. Stevenson has observed, "My work with the poor and incarcerated has persuaded me that the opposite of poverty is not wealth; the opposite of poverty is justice."

In more recent years, Stevenson has focused on the history of American slavery and southern lynchings in the post-Reconstruction era. He says, "Truth and reconciliation have always been sequential. You can't get to reconciliation and recovery until you've got to the truth, and we've not done a very good job of telling the truth."

EJI's National Memorial for Peace and Justice and the Legacy Museum: From Enslavement to Mass Incarceration both opened in 2018. The memorial is a place to honor the lives of those who were lynched across the South. The museum focuses on African American history through the lenses of American slavery, Jim Crow, and the criminal justice system. Stevenson also coordinates with towns throughout the South to gather soil and erect memorial markers where atrocities occurred. "We've created the counter-narrative that says we have nothing about which we should be ashamed."

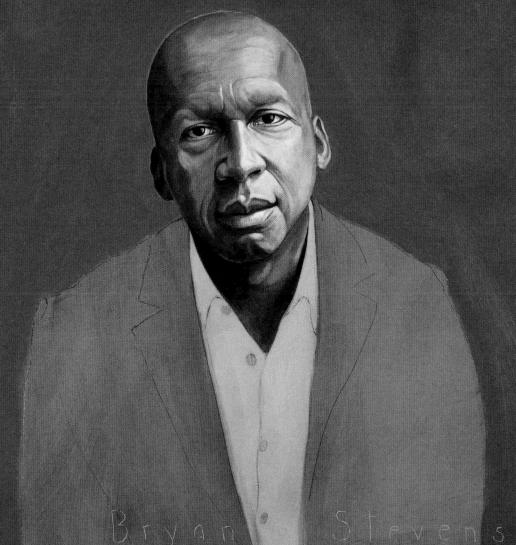

The great evil of American slavery was not involuntary servitude but rather the narrative of racial differences we created to legitimate slavery. Because we never dealt with that evil, I don't think slavery ended in 1865, it just evolved.

Bryan Stevenson

Robert Shetterly 2017

Emma Tenayuca

Organizer; b. 1916, d. 1999

I was arrested a number of times. . . . I never thought in terms of fear. I thought in terms of justice.

Born in 1916 in San Antonio, Texas, Emma Tenayuca lived at a time when Mexican Americans were allowed few freedoms and fewer privileges. Her close relationship with a grandfather who read the newspapers with her and took her to rallies for the rights of the poor fed the young girl's profound hunger for both learning and social justice.

At age sixteen, already determined to challenge injustice, she became involved in community organizing and was jailed and threatened numerous times. At a time when neither Mexican Americans nor women were expected to speak out, she spoke out fearlessly and was soon known as a fiery orator and brilliant organizer.

By age twenty-one, Emma was considered to be one of the most effective organizers for the Workers Alliance of America. That same year, 1938, when San Antonio's lowest-paid workers suffered massive wage cuts, they decided to strike. The city's twelve thousand pecan shellers, most of them women, elected Emma to lead their strike. In less than two months, the pecan shellers forced the owners to raise their pay. The pecan shellers' strike is considered by many historians to be the first significant victory in the Mexican American struggle for political and economic equality in this country.

Emma was so articulate and outspoken that the Workers Alliance replaced her when she was twenty-two. There was only so much room for a woman—a Mexican woman—to be an ambitious and intellectual champion for justice.

In 1939, as Emma was giving a speech, an enraged mob attacked San Antonio's Municipal Auditorium. Fearing that she would be lynched, Emma was led away through a secret passageway. The mob threw bricks, broke windows, set fires, ripped out auditorium seats, and later that night, together with the Ku Klux Klan, burned the city's mayor in effigy for having defended Emma's right to free speech. This event is still on record as San Antonio's largest riot.

Blacklisted, Emma left the state for many years, suffering poverty, unemployment, and personal threats against her safety. A voracious reader, she put herself through college and never stopped searching for an answer to the injustices she saw around her.

In the 1960s, Emma returned to San Antonio and began a different phase of her lifelong community service, becoming a reading teacher for migrant students. Emma always focused on empowering people in the most basic and humane ways, inspiring and supporting their ability to work, to eat, to feed their families, to read, to vote. The things she fought to achieve in our society—Social Security, unemployment benefits, minimum wage, equal access to education, disability benefits—were in her days labeled "Communist." Today, they are considered to be markers of social justice.

Although scorned by her detractors, among the people for whom she fought and sacrificed, her name was whispered with a respect reserved for no other leader. They called her "La Pasionaria de Texas."

Emma Tenayuca

I was arrested a number of times ...
I never thought in terms of fear.
I thought in terms of justice.

Robert Shetterly 2008

Sojourner Truth

Abolitionist, evangelist, feminist; b. circa 1797, d. 1883

*Now I hears talkin' about de Constitution and de rights of man. I comes up and takes
hold of dis Constitution. It looks mighty big, and I feels for my rights, but der aint any dare.
Den I says, God, what ails dis Constitution? He says to me, "Sojourner, der is a little weasel in it."*

Sojourner Truth was one of those rare, remarkable individuals who rise far above their intended station in life. What future could have been expected for a Black female slave born into a nation controlled by free white men? Truth grew up with no schooling and was unable to read or write. Who could have imagined that she would become one of America's greatest orators or that she would produce (through dictation to a neighbor) one of the nineteenth century's most inspirational autobiographies?

Not much is known about Truth's early years. Originally called Isabella, she was born at the end of the 1790s to slave parents owned by a wealthy Dutch family in Ulster County, New York. As a teenager working for a different household nearby in New Paltz (this section of New Paltz is now in the town of Esopus), she bore five children to a fellow slave, at least three of whom were sold and sent away from her.

After sixteen years in New Paltz, Isabella escaped in 1826 by fleeing to a Quaker family. By the time she reached New York City, three years later, the state had decreed the emancipation of slaves, allowing her to stop running and hiding. Working as a servant, she became involved with various religious movements; in 1843, feeling that God had called her "to travel up and down the land, showing the people their sins and being a sign to them," she renamed herself Sojourner Truth.

At six feet tall, Truth's commanding presence was complemented by a tremendous natural charisma. Her speeches were direct but clever, delivered in Dutch-accented English. Truth became a powerful voice against racial oppression and, later, for the women's suffrage movement. In 1851, at a women's rights convention in Ohio, she gave her most famous speech, in which she repeatedly asked, "Ain't I a woman?" Her words were not formally recorded until twelve years later, when Frances Gage, president of the convention, set down her gripping account of the speech.

In a long article for the April 1863 issue of *The Atlantic Monthly*, Harriet Beecher Stowe wrote, "I do not recollect ever to have been conversant with any one who had more of that silent and subtle power which we call personal presence . . . [Truth] seemed perfectly self-possessed and at her ease. . . . An audience was what she wanted—it mattered not whether high or low, learned or ignorant. She had things to say, and was ready to say them at all times, and to any one."

Sojourner Truth traveled as an itinerant preacher for about ten years. Then, after a brief time in Battle Creek, Michigan, she moved to nearby Harmonia, a utopian community, in 1857, where she remained for the next decade. In 1867, she returned to Battle Creek for the remaining years of her life. Her funeral there in 1883 was the largest that town had ever seen.

Sojourner   Truth

Now I hears talkin' about de Constitution and de rights of man.
I comes up and takes hold of dis Constitution It looks mighty
big, and I feels for my rights, but der aint any dare. Den I
says, God, what ails dis Constitution? He says to me,
"Sojourner, der is a little weasel in it."

Harriet Tubman

Underground Railroad conductor, social reformer, nurse, spy; b. circa 1820, d. 1913

I started with this idea in my head, There's two things I've got a right to,
and these are, Death or Liberty—one or the other I mean to have.

The hundreds of slaves she helped to freedom and the thousands of others she inspired called her "Moses." Harriet Tubman became the most famous leader of the Underground Railroad, an elaborate and secret series of houses, tunnels, and roads set up by abolitionists and former slaves to aid slaves escaping from slave states to free states and Canada.

Harriet Tubman was born into slavery as Araminta Ross in Bucktown, Maryland, in the early 1820s. After her owner died, fearing that she would be sold farther south, Tubman escaped to Philadelphia in 1849. "When I had found that I had crossed the line, I looked at my hands to see if I was the same person," she later said. "[T]he sun came like gold through the trees, and over the field, and I felt like I was in Heaven."

After her escape, Tubman worked as a maid in Philadelphia and joined the city's large abolitionist group. In 1850, after Congress passed the Fugitive Slave Act, making it illegal to help a runaway slave, Tubman joined the Underground Railroad. During her first expedition, in December 1850, she managed to thread her way through the backwoods to Baltimore and return north with her niece and her niece's children. From that time until the onset of the Civil War, Tubman traveled to the South at least eighteen times and enabled the escape of close to three hundred slaves. In 1857, she led her parents to freedom. After a brief time in Ontario, they settled in Auburn, New York, which became her home, as well. Tubman oversaw every aspect of each escape—planning the route, dispensing drugs to quiet babies, and carrying a gun for protection and to threaten any fearful runaway who wanted to turn back, saying, "You'll be free or die." As her reputation grew, rewards for her capture in the South reached as high as forty thousand dollars.

During the Civil War, Tubman served as a nurse, scout, and spy for the Union army. She took part in a military campaign that resulted in the rescue of more than seven hundred slaves.

After the war, Tubman returned to Auburn and continued her involvement in social issues, including women's rights. In 1908, when she finally received some of the veteran's pay denied her for thirty years, she established a home in Auburn for elderly and indigent Blacks that later became known as the Harriet Tubman House. She died there on March 10, 1913.

I started with this idea in my head. There's two things I've got a right to, and these are, Death or Liberty — one or the other I mean to have.

Moses

Harriet Tubman

Robert Shetterly 2004

Gladys Vega

Executive director, La Colaborativa; b. 1967

There's a long history of institutions and nonprofits being led by people who do not reflect the communities being served. White decision makers would come into our communities and let us know what we needed. We know that this doesn't work, it never has. Representation matters. It is time for people of color to make decisions for themselves and their own communities. We must be seen and heard. La Colaborativa protects, uplifts, and empowers every individual to foster leadership from within communities of color and immigrant communities. This is the only way that real change can happen.

At the age of nine, Gladys Vega moved with her family from Puerto Rico to Chelsea, Massachusetts, where she witnessed firsthand the challenges facing Latinos in the United States. She saw gentrification displace residents, economic opportunity bypass her neighbors, and deportation destroy families. Using the tools of democracy and human rights—voter registration, economic development, legislative reform, educational opportunity—she was determined to bring justice, equality, and opportunity to her community.

In 1990, Vega joined the Chelsea Collaborative, a local nonprofit advocating for immigrants' rights. There she worked in whatever capacity the moment required, fighting for tenants' rights, working to create positive connections between law enforcement and residents, advocating for the poor, and helping Chelsea youths find summer jobs. Vega's passion, professionalism, and impeccable organizing won her the trust and admiration of her community, and in 2006 she became the Chelsea Collaborative's executive director. Under her leadership, the organization has been renamed La Colaborativa to better reflect its mission.

Vega's tenure began with characteristic tenacity. She urged the City Council to make Chelsea the third sanctuary city in Massachusetts. She gave her time to Centro Latino, the Chelsea Board of Health, and the United Way Committee. She served as a Democratic delegate for the National Convention in 2000. In 2007 and 2008, she was named one of the state's one hundred most influential leaders.

Then came COVID-19, and the city's status as home to a large population of undocumented immigrants took on an entirely new meaning. Living in compact housing units served by outdated ventilation systems, Latinos contracted the deadly disease at an alarming rate. The community members' need to work outside the home further exposed them in the workplace and on public transportation. Chelsea's many undocumented immigrants were shut out of the means of assistance, such as health care and stimulus checks.

Vega and La Colaborativa stepped up to assume the work the government either couldn't or wouldn't do. She collected financial and material donations, turning her office into a pantry where residents could pick up supplies. Local bodegas, uncertain of their own ability to keep their doors open, gave food. "A man on Social Security gave me ten dollars," Vega said. "It's been the most beautiful show of poor people helping poor people."

Vega's work over the years set a model for her neighbors and showed them the power of acting as a community, and while COVID-19 has set Chelsea back, Vega continues efforts to empower her city and ensure that the Latino community assumes the lead in determining its own needs. She believes empowerment of the individual leads to empowerment of the community as the ethnically and culturally rich place it is.

There's a long history of institutions and nonprofits being led by people who do not reflect the communities being served. White decision makers would come into our communities and let us know what we needed. We know that this doesn't work, it never has. Representation matters. It is time for people of color to make decisions for themselves and their own communities. We must be seen and heard.

La Colaborativa protects, uplifts, and empowers every individual to foster leadership from within communities of color and immigrant communities. This is the only way that that real change can happen.

Gladys Vega

Robit Shetterly 2020

Ida B. Wells

Journalist, antilynching crusader, women's rights advocate; b. 1862, d. 1931

I'd rather go down in history as one lone Negro who dared to tell the government
that it had done a dastardly thing than to save my skin by taking back what I have said.

Ida B. Wells was born into slavery in Holly Springs, Mississippi, just months prior to emancipation in 1863. Her parents died of yellow fever when she was sixteen, and Wells, though minimally educated, began teaching to support her five younger siblings. She somehow managed to keep her family together, attend Shaw University (now Rust College), and secure a teaching position in Memphis.

When she was twenty-one, traveling in Tennessee, Wells defied a conductor's order to move to a segregated railroad car and was forcibly removed. She won a lawsuit against the railroad (which was later reversed) and, from that point on, worked tirelessly to overcome injustices to people of color and to women. In 1889, she became co-owner of a Memphis newspaper, the *Free Speech and Headlight*. Her editorials protesting the lynching of three Black friends led to a boycott of white businesses, the destruction of her newspaper office, and threats against her life. Undeterred, she carried her antilynching crusade to Chicago and published *Southern Horrors: Lynch Law in All Its Phases* (1892), documenting racial lynching in America.

In 1895, when she married Ferdinand L. Barnett, attorney and owner of *The Conservator*, Chicago's first Black newspaper, she hyphenated her name, making it Wells-Barnett. Though married and eventually the mother of four children, Wells-Barnett continued to write and organize. She was a founder of the National Association for the Advancement of Colored People (NAACP), marched in the parade for universal suffrage in Washington, D.C. (1913), and established the Negro Fellowship League for Black men and the first kindergarten for Black children in Chicago.

Wells did not succeed in her crusade to get Congress to pass antilynching laws during her lifetime, but her efforts as a writer and activist dedicated to justice and social change established her as one of the most forceful and remarkable women of her time. Ida B. Wells died in Chicago. She once said, "One had better die fighting against injustice than die like a dog or a rat in a trap."

I'd rather go down in history as one lone Negro who dared to tell the government that it had done a dastardly thing than to save my skin by taking back what I have said

Ida B Wells

Carter Woodson

Educator, historian, author; b. 1875, d. 1950

If you teach the Negro that he has accomplished as much good as any other race,
he will aspire to equality and justice without regard to race. Such an effort would
upset the program of the oppressor in both Africa and America.

"If a race has no history, if it has no worthwhile tradition, it becomes a negligible factor in the thought of the world, and it stands in danger of being exterminated," Woodson wrote. Recognizing that the African American experience was ignored in U.S. history written in the seventeenth and eighteenth centuries, he took as his life's work the recording of African American contributions.

Woodson was born in New Canton, Virginia, on December 19, 1875, to James and Anne Woodson—both former slaves. The family moved to West Virginia, where Woodson found work as a coal miner and the opportunity to gain an education. When Woodson was nearly twenty, he enrolled in Frederick Douglass High School in Huntington, West Virginia, and graduated in two years. In 1903, he earned a bachelor's degree from Berea College, the South's first racially integrated and coeducational institution of higher learning. After teaching in the Philippines from 1903 to 1907, and then earning a second bachelor's degree and a master's degree in European history at the University of Chicago, Woodson completed his formal education at Harvard University, where he earned a Ph.D. in history, becoming the second African American—and the only one born to former slaves—to earn a Ph.D. from Harvard (W. E. B. Du Bois was the first).

While teaching high school in Washington, D.C., in 1915, Woodson cofounded the Association for the Study of Negro Life and History (now the Association for the Study of African American Life and History). That same year, Woodson's first book, *The Education of the Negro Prior to 1861*, was published. The following year, Woodson founded *The Journal of Negro History* (now *The Journal of African American History*).

Woodson also traveled across the country, holding conferences, mentoring young historians, publishing more articles and books, and collecting source materials to preserve African American history. In 1921, he established Associated Publishers, among the nation's oldest African American publishing houses, to promote African American writers. And in 1926, Woodson promoted "Negro History Week," choosing the second week of February because it corresponded with the birthdays of Frederick Douglass and Abraham Lincoln. Fifty years later, this became Black History Month.

In his most enduring publication, *The Mis-Education of the Negro*, published in 1933, Woodson argued that American education reinforced the inferiority of African Americans and wholly ignored their contributions. "The oppressor has always indoctrinated the weak with his interpretation of the crimes of the strong," he wrote. "[T]o handicap a student by teaching him that his black face is a curse and that his struggle to change his condition is hopeless is the worst sort of lynching."

Through his academic work, as well as his participation in many prominent African American organizations, Woodson was very much a creator of the zeitgeist that caused African American history and culture to flourish in the early twentieth century, earning him the title "Father of Black History."

If you teach the Negro that he has accomplished as much good as any other race, he will aspire to equality and justice without regard to race. Such an effort would upset the program of the oppressor in Africa and America.

Carter G. Woodson

Malcolm X, El Hajj Malik el Shabazz

Black Nationalist, Muslim leader; b. 1925, d. 1965

We're not Americans, we're Africans who happen to be in America. We were kidnapped and brought here against our will from Africa. We didn't land on Plymouth rock—that rock landed on us.

Malcolm X was born Malcolm Little in Omaha, Nebraska. His father, Earl, a Baptist minister and follower of the Black Nationalist Marcus Garvey, was under continuous threat from the Ku Klux Klan. The family moved to Lansing, Michigan, where their house was burned by white racists in 1929, and in 1931, Earl was purportedly murdered by white racists. A few years later, Malcolm's mother suffered a nervous breakdown, and her seven children were sent to various foster homes.

The top student and only African American in his eighth-grade class, Malcolm dropped out of school after his teacher told him that a "nigger" could never become a lawyer—his dream. He went to Boston to live with his sister Ella and turned to crime. He became a street hustler and, in 1946, was arrested and sentenced to eight to ten years in prison. While incarcerated, he began a period of education and self-transformation. He later joined the Nation of Islam, a Black supremacist group headed by Elijah Muhammad. He took X as his last name, signifying his unknown African tribal name, which had been lost when his family was given the slave name Little.

After his parole, in 1952, Malcolm X became a brilliant and charismatic speaker, building the Nation of Islam from four hundred members to thirty thou-

sand. In 1964, he broke with the Nation of Islam and in 1965 formed the Organization of Afro-American Unity. Journeying to Mecca, the holiest of Muslim cities, he took the name El Hajj Malik el Shabazz and began speaking of international Black consciousness and integration, rather than racial separatism. His change of view targeted him for assassination by some members of the Nation of Islam.

While preparing to speak in Harlem's Audubon Ballroom on February 21, 1965, Malcolm X was shot and killed. Three men from the Nation of Islam were arrested for his murder. It is still unclear what role the New York City Police Department and the FBI, which had Malcolm X under surveillance, may have played in his death.

Historians consider Malcolm X among the half dozen most influential African American leaders. *The Autobiography of Malcolm X,* written with Alex Haley and published posthumously, is considered one of the most important nonfiction books of the twentieth century. Many Black people felt that Malcolm X, by voicing the truth of their frustration and anger, gave them courage and self-respect. He told African Americans that they had to stop defining themselves as whites had defined them—as subservient and inferior. His message was one of strength, pride, and truth.

Malcolm X
El Hajj Malik el Shabazz

We're not Americans, we're Africans who happen to be in America. We were kidnapped and brought here against our will from Africa. We didn't land on Plymouth rock — that rock landed on us.

Robert Shetterly 2004

Rev. Lennox Yearwood, Jr.

Civil rights and climate activist; b. 1969

100 years from now none of us will be here. But what will be here is the spirit of us fighting for a just, sustainable, prosperous world for all. We fight not only for ourselves but for future generations. Power to the people!"

Climate change and hip-hop have been brought into radical convergence by the Reverend Lennox Yearwood, Jr., president and CEO of the Hip Hop Caucus and an elder in the Church of God in Christ (COGIC), where he is known as "the Rev." Yearwood harnesses the revolutionary global music phenomenon to engage the world's most pressing crisis.

Yearwood's parents immigrated to Shreveport, Louisiana, from Trinidad and Tobago, then moved to Washington, D.C., where Yearwood grew up. After earning his undergraduate degree, Yearwood earned a M.Div. degree from Howard University School of Divinity in 2002, then completed the Chaplain Candidate Program with the U.S. Air Force Reserve in 2003.

While in the air force, Yearwood began working with hip-hop mogul Russell Simmons. In 2004, Yearwood founded the Hip Hop Caucus, an organization focused on "mo-vote-bilizing" the hip-hop generation into political action. "To 'hip' means to inform, to 'hop' means to cause to move, and to 'caucus' means to do it together." Yearwood and the Hip Hop Caucus work with high-profile hip-hop artists on voter registration and get-out-the-vote drives, "us[ing] our cultural expression to shape our political experience. This is how we make voting, to some degree, sexy . . . [and] fun."

Yearwood zeroed in on the relationship between the changing climate and vulnerable African American communities during the aftermath of Hurricane Katrina. While serving as the national director of the Gulf Coast Renewal Campaign, it became clear to him that "the biggest target of Climate Change and pollution is communities of color, because polluters have been able to locate their facilities in our communities by promising jobs that never come to fruition and lying about the deadly health impacts of their pollution." He says, "Climate change is our [Woolworth's] lunch counter moment for the 21st century."

While still serving as a U.S. Air Force Reserve chaplain, Yearwood organized the 2007 concert tour "Make Hip Hop Not War" to protest the U.S. presence in Iraq. Six days after announcing the tour, he received notification from the air force that he was being honorably discharged on the basis of "behavior clearly inconsistent with the interest of national security."

While supporting a 100 percent clean energy future that benefits the health of the planet and the health of the economy, Yearwood builds a big tent. "It is time," he says, "for America to unleash its entrepreneurial can-do spirit through a war-time like mobilization to help save America, and the world." Yearwood cheered the action of the "Water Protectors" of Standing Rock, saying, "They led a spiritual movement based in love, prayer and peace, fortified by culture, the wisdom of the elders and courage of youth alike." That spirit of unity is what Yearwood brings to the table: "[W]e must come together as human beings fighting for justice."

100 years from now, none of us will be here. But what will be here is the spirit of us fighting for a just, sustainable, and prosperous world for all. We fight not only for ourselves, but for future generations.
All power to the people!

Rev. Lennox Yearwood

Dave Zirin

Sports journalist; b. 1973

Racism is not about hurtful words, bruised feelings, political correctness, or refusing to call short people "'vertically challenged." Racism is about the power to treat entire groups of people as something less than human—for the benefit of that power. That's why a Native American sports mascot is far from harmless.

In his 2011 book, *Game Over*, Dave Zirin concluded that Americans are being robbed by the owners of sports teams. "Now when many of us see the local stadium, we see a $1 billion real estate leviathan . . . that . . . has created a new species of fan: those who are paying for the stadiums [through taxes] but, unless they are working behind a counter, are unable to enter their gates."

Zirin was born and raised in New York City. Like many boys and girls in America, he grew up participating in organized sports and following his local teams: the Knicks, Mets, and Rangers. One of his favorite players was New York Giants linebacker Lawrence Taylor, a man who revolutionized the position with his athletic and aggressive play.

Some years later, in 1996, the story of an NBA player named Mahmoud Abdul-Rauf caught Zirin's attention. Abdul-Rauf refused to come out of the locker room for the playing of the national anthem, objecting to the use of sports for nationalistic ends. He said that the flag may represent freedom and democracy to some, but to others it represents tyranny and oppression. Abdul-Rauf's career was short-lived.

Zirin listened to the talking heads on ESPN say that Abdul-Rauf must be one of those activist athletes, like Billie Jean King, Muhammad Ali, or Arthur Ashe. He wondered what an "athlete activist" was, so he started researching. This moment changed his career. He was deeply influenced by Howard Zinn's *A People's History of the United States* and would go on to write *A People's History of Sports in the United States*.

As a pioneering sports journalist, Zirin began to challenge readers to think about the connection between sports and social and economic justice. He came to realize that you can't talk about the American civil rights movement without mentioning Jackie Robinson or Muhammad Ali, or about gay rights without talking about Billie Jean King and Martina Navratilova.

Zirin writes of the "plantation overseer" dynamic found in college and professional athletics in the United States and sees the racism in sports as an extension of the larger society's culture: "If we accept that racism is still alive and well outside the arena, then sports would have to exist in a hermetically sealed, airtight environment in order to remain uninfected. Impossible."

Zirin has analyzed the links between Teddy Roosevelt, Muscular Christianity, and military invasions of the Philippines, Latin American, and the Caribbean. "[Sports] has always been about selling a supremely militaristic, dominant image of the United States back to ourselves. After all, who tossed the coin at the 2009 Super Bowl? It wasn't John Elway or Joe Montana. It was General David Petraeus."

As of 2020, Zirin has written ten books, made two movies, and contributed to numerous magazines, including *The Nation*, *SLAM* magazine, and *The Progressive*. He also publishes a blog called Edge of Sports.

Dave Zirin

Racism is not about hurtful words, bruised feelings, political correctness, or refusing to call short people "vertically challenged." Racism is about the power to treat entire groups of people as something less than human — for the benefit of that power. That's why a Native American sports mascot is far from harmless.

Acknowledgments

The *Americans Who Tell the Truth* portrait project began as a solitary endeavor, an act of art therapy to help me reconcile with the violent hypocrisies of this country's difficult history. Its success, however, has been due to the many people who have contributed in so many ways to its expansion and educational mission, people who have helped to shape it into a project far greater than I could have ever imagined.

AWTT began and is still, at its core, an art project. My belief in the power of art to focus attention, to inspire, to enrich, and to teach is based in great part in the quality of art. I often say that good art authenticates its own message. If people recognize the quality of the work, they are likely to give credence to its message. Each portrait carries an ethical or political message, but prior to the message, I attempt to make a good painting and honor the person with as good a likeness as I can manage, and find something essential about the person with the paint. The extent to which I am successful is due in large part to the critical advice of my partner, Gail Page, also an artist, whose advice I seek at various stages of every portrait. I could not possibly exaggerate my gratitude for her willingness to tell me the truth when I was struggling with a likeness, even when I may not have been keen to hear it.

For many years now, a core team has made most of the decisions about the implementation of our mission and the formulation of our educational work—my son, Aran Shetterly, executive director; Connie Carter, our education director; and I. Aran and Connie have been totally dedicated to this project. They combine creativity and wisdom with practicality. My gratitude is immense. As much as the portrait subjects, they have been my teachers.

Central to our mission is matching an inspiring narrative with each portrait. Over the years we've had a great team of researchers/writers. These include Anne Cushman, Rachel Mack, Jeffrey Harris, Julie Gronlund, Richard Sassaman, Adrienne Chamberlin, Daegan Miller, and Laura Rothstein. And in preparation for this book, the bios had to be edited down to half their length. This was done by Kathleen Caldwell, who also does a lot of the management of the AWTT website.

I want to thank a few of the strong advocates for AWTT over the years who have arranged exhibits and worked hard to increase our impact: Jim Clark, Kate Laissle, Julia Ganson, Rose Viviano, Michele Hemenway, Laura Rothstein, Joe Gutmann, Nancy Doda, and Argy Nestor. Jim Clark, for more than eight years, has promoted the inclusion of AWTT in the curriculum of Syracuse University and arranged the only, to this point, exhibit of the entire collection at SU in 2018. Michele Hemenway, from Louisville, was the first teacher to begin building an AWTT curriculum for her classroom in 2004 and has worked with us ever since.

I want to mention Ellie Richard from Asheville, North Carolina, and Meryl Baier of Ipswich, Massachusetts, and a team of volunteers from Charlottesville, Virginia (Julie Gronlund, Bruce Gordon, Linda Winecoff, Emma Terry, Jacqueline Langholtz, Lynne Levine, Catherine Spear, Michael Spear, Andrea Douglas, Enid Krieger). They pioneered novel ways of engaging entire communities in participation with AWTT exhibits.

These people as staff and board members have made invaluable contributions to the viability of AWTT: Bob Sargent, Scott Gardiner, Rachel Freedman, Marion Morris, Sherry Streeter, Dud Hendrick, Betty Burkes, Jamie Kilbreth, and Charlie Clements.

I want to thank my daughter Caitlin Shetterly for her advice and moral support.

I want to thank Dumitru Ciubatii for his wonderful design of our website, Ken Woisard for his excellent photography of the portraits, and J. S. McCarthy Printers for their beautiful reproductions.

Thank you to all the schools and other organizations that have hosted exhibitions and engaged with our curriculum. And thank you to all the people who have supported this project with donations and purchases of cards and posters.

A special thanks to Lynne Elizabeth, our publisher at New Village Press, who believed in the project and made the book happen. She's been a delight to work with.

Lastly, I want to offer my immense gratitude to the portrait subjects themselves. Democracy, justice, and equality do not happen because of our founding documents. They happen because people like those I've painted insist they are made real for everyone. Their dedication and courage, the truths they tell, the risks they take, make our ideals real.

My apologies to the thousands of others I have not been able to paint. Someone else will have to do that.